A View from
the Street

a View from THE STREET

Donald T. Regan

NEW AMERICAN LIBRARY

TIMES MIRROR

NEW YORK

Library of Congress Catalog Card Number: 77-185020

Published by The New American Library, Inc.
1301 Avenue of the Americas, New York, New York 10019

Published simultaneously in Canada by
George McLeod, Ltd., Toronto

Distributed by W. W. Norton & Company, Inc.
55 Fifth Avenue, New York, New York 10003

First Printing 1972

PRINTED IN THE UNITED STATES OF AMERICA

FOR ANN

CONTENTS

FOREWORD

THE PAST, THE PRESENT AND THE IMMEDIATE future on Wall Street doubtless constitute one of the most exciting—not to say the most difficult—periods in the Street's long and colorful history. The daily journals and the weekly news magazines have poured out facts and opinions about the dramatic events of 1970 and 1971. Indeed, at one point virtually everybody in the United States had some comments, most of them critical, to make about the people and the events on the Street. Congress has discussed, and continues to discuss, the affairs of Wall Street with new interest and intensity. The Securities and Exchange Commission has launched extensive hearings, which test the endurance of witnesses and Commission alike.

The financial world will never be the same as a result of this experience. From it will emerge financial institutions far different from those that governed in the epoch that ended in 1968. We are headed, it appears, toward a new Securities Act of 1972 or 1973, which will supplement in an important way the Acts of 1933 and 1934—the legislative cornerstones on which the present industry is built.

Despite all this voluminous attention given to the news from the Street, I am persuaded that no one has yet fully understood the importance to the future of the events so recently past. No one has described those events completely, accurately, or with the meticulous precision that, historically, they warrant. One of my purposes in writing this book is to accomplish that end—to set down, in one continuous narrative, the story of Wall Street's recent wild years. As chief operating officer and then as chairman and chief executive of Merrill Lynch, Pierce, Fenner & Smith Inc., I was both witness to and participant in what I regard as being great events. It is not immodest to claim that I played some small part in the shaping of those events: mine was only one of many voices, but in accordance with my lifelong propensity, I had no hesitancy in speaking out, and I even managed to be heard now and again.

But there is a second purpose here as well. In essence, this is two books. One, as I have indicated, recounts the chronology of events on Wall Street in 1970 and 1971, accompanied

ix

by appropriate and, I hope, interesting remarks and explications. With that as background, the second book attempts to discern and limn the shape of the future. While risk is always involved in any such process, in this case it is not quite to be equated with gazing into a crystal ball. Forces are at work changing the Street. Many of them are readily recognizable. In many respects, their impact is at least generally predictable by someone who has spent his life studying them. We are facing change, but we are not leaping into the unknown.

Lurking here may even be a third book—at least, a series of rather lengthy complicated definitions. The jargon of the Street is not always comprehensible to outsiders. Indeed, many of our terms are not clearly defined or precisely understood even by ourselves. When people in the securities industry speak of "the money supply," or "free credit balances," or "fails," or "member firm's capital," we are not always absolutely certain what we mean. Nor, of course, can we be certain that whomever we are engaging in conversation—even though he may be a member of the industry and have long experience in it—understands the terms to mean exactly what we intend them to mean. I have, therefore, set out some working definitions which seem to me to be clarifying, both to those of us who travel daily to this part of the jungle and to those who find it a nice place to visit but wouldn't want to live here. They are contained in the lengthy Glossary beginning on page 191.

What I am putting forth in this book—if you will, in these three books—are my personal views. I do not speak here for Merrill Lynch. Neither have I set out to write a company history, to formulate company policy, or to write a piece of puffery about the firm—good though I believe it to be. The book is innocent of press-agentry. I have simply gratified my own wish to communicate my experiences and opinions of the last couple of years. I am also moved to write, in part, by the recent spate of books that make Wall Street sound as though it were the meeting place of pirates and con men. Pirates and con men do walk along the Street. But they do not permanently belong to its constituency.

In the course of this book, I will have a great deal to say about the markets—stock markets, bond markets, money markets, and, indeed, the overall concept of the marketplace in our free enterprise system. Markets move in mysterious ways, and there are no means of predicting exactly what direction they will take. None of my comments is to be construed as in any way a market forecast. Obviously, my own business judgments and decisions are based on what I believe is going to happen. Like Merrill Lynch, I am bullish on America. But no one should act on the basis of my estimate of the future.

Donald T. Regan

ACKNOWLEDGMENTS

IN THE COURSE OF WRITING THIS BOOK, I, LIKE most authors, took full advantage of the forebearance of my family, the kindness of my associates, and the competence of several people within and outside of the ambit of my working life.

My first indebtedness is to my wife, who lived with considerable patience and understanding through two broken vacations while this book was under construction. For that reason and many others, I am dedicating the book to her.

Also, I have a kind of collective obligation to my colleagues at Merrill Lynch. We lived together through the periods described here, and many of the judgments I arrived at grew out of my almost continuous discussions with them—although the judgments are my own. I had many stimulating conversations with Ned B. Ball, Merrill Lynch's president. Another close associate, Walter Guzzardi Jr.—a vice president of Merrill Lynch, an author, and formerly assistant managing editor of *Fortune*—lent me invaluable assistance by his editing and his critical evaluations of the several versions of the manuscript.

I am also indebted to Richard Whalen for his thoughts on the relationships between Wall Street and Washington; to Lea Guyer, Barney Freeman, Robert L. Tebeau, Elizabeth Gibson, and Linda Ripinsky for their research efforts through various drafts; to Richard Callanan of the New York Stock Exchange for his historical knowledge; and to Mary Grace for her careful proofreading.

A View from
the Street

CHAPTER I

Three Days in May

SOME MOMENTS IN HISTORY SEEM TO SUM UP
and typify much longer passages of time. A critical year can
catch up a decade, and some decades seem to tell the story of
a century. Three days in May 1970—May 25, May 26, and
May 27—had that very special quality about them. They told
the story of 1970, and forecast much of 1971 as well. In a
sense, they were the past, the present and the future. They
were the days that had everything. To take them apart, to
analyze their eventful hours, to trace back causes to their
roots, is to be led to big issues—issues political, military,
psychological, financial and educational, which were dogging
and deviling the country for two critically important years of
the Nixon Administration. They are grand issues, and many
of them—along with the need to resolve them—are with us
still. Their dimensions have not been reduced by time.

The place where much of the action centered, the narrow
field in which the big flurry was concentrated, was Wall Street.
There have been times before when Wall Street—a dirty, over-
grown, and overbuilt section of downtown Manhattan—stood
as the geographical center for nationwide emotions. The Street
is analogous to the epicenter of an earthquake. At some of
history's great moments, anyway, what people *feel* has a
direct effect on what they do with their possessions. Under
heavy pressure, they may or may not buy or sell their houses—
but they are very likely to buy or sell securities. Whether they
act out of a sense of impotence or defiance or self-protection I
do not know, but buy and sell at an increased rate they certainly do when under the stress of great events. A hot war, a
freeze on wages and prices, an assassination, the end of a labor
dispute—for reasons that will never be fully understood, these

17

events make people into traders. Affected and infected by the climate of excitement, they hurry to buy, hurry to sell.

And buy and sell they did on May 25, 26 and 27, 1970, days that wrote new records into the chronicles of financial history. On May 25, half of the 1,800 stocks listed on the New York Exchange hit their low prices for the year until that time. That means, in the old platitude of the Street, that sellers must have outnumbered buyers, and on May 25 they surely did. The day started out, metaphorically, with two sellers chasing one buyer, and it looked as though it ended with ten chasing one. Good stocks, indifferent stocks and poor stocks all hit the skids. IBM, a great company, dropped that day by $7.00 a share—a paper loss of $802,108,762. Walt Disney, one of the leading growth stocks of the 1960s, dropped more than $6.00, a paper loss of $34,427,472. Other equally good names did just as poorly: American Research and Development, Owens-Corning Fiberglas, Bausch & Lomb. It was a day for the bears.

Still, on May 25 nobody was speaking aloud that terrible word—crash. Any definition of the word is highly subjective, but the word wasn't heard at the time, and it is not used descriptively in retrospect, either. Only about 12.6-million shares changed hands on May 25, and while by the lights of 1950 that was a good deal of volume, it was not extremely heavy for 1970. By the standards of the present it was, I suppose, what the columnists would call a "moderately active" day. The daily average number of shares traded in 1969 was 11,403,000, while the average for the first four months of 1970 was 10,500,000 shares. So, as you can see, nobody had hit the panic button—not at that point on May 25.

Yet gloom hung like pollution over the Street. The Dow Jones Industrial Average (**G**) fell steadily on May 25, finally ending up at 641.36, a one-day drop of 20.81 points. When the gong (**G**) sounded that day, the Dow Jones' final resting place (**G**)* was lower than it had been since President Kennedy was assassinated on November 22, 1963. But when trad-

---

* I note that I have already used three terms that may need some explaining to the lay reader. People who have spent their lives in the securities industry, as I have, put on a business vocabulary the way a cleric puts on his habit in the morning. The cleric, I would guess, very rapidly forgets that he is not dressed like other men; similarly, the day-time residents of Wall Street forget that often they do not sound like other men. Explanations and historical notes about such terms as Dow Jones Industrials, the gong, and selling climax begin on p. 191. All terms so explained are marked in the text by a boldface (**G**). They are arranged alphabetically.

ing, to everyone's great relief, finally did cease at 3:30 P.M. on May 25, Wall Street felt it had not yet witnessed one of its most fearful orgies—the selling climax (**G**).

When trading ended on Monday night, May 25, nobody knew whether the stock market had hit bottom. But everybody was perfectly sure on the evidence that the market had been looking for the bottom. The drop in the Dow Jones was only one of the many indications of that. The number of declining stocks outnumbered those that advanced by 1,370 to 130, or by 10-to-1. Of the 1,370 stocks that declined, 911 of them hit what were then their lows for the year.

When we talk about stock averages going up and down, we use the word "points." But that is a euphemism. What we are talking about, of course, are dollars. With a delicacy that it does not show in many other respects, Wall Street always says "a point and a quarter" when it might just as well say "$1.25," or it says "5/8ths" when it means simply "62½ cents."* So that drop of 20 points in the Dow Jones—and with respect to the Dow Jones we are speaking about averages, so "points" is correct, and they are not translatable into dollars on a one for one basis—meant in fact a decline in the value of those 30 leading securities by $2,477,000,000. To the $15,-350,000,000 in losses suffered by stocks listed on the New York Stock Exchange, and nearly $1-billion on the American Stock Exchange (**G**), must be added the uncalculated billions lost in the over-the-counter (**G**) market. On the record books, anyway, the nation went to bed that night countless billions of dollars poorer than it was when it woke up that morning. The national mood, none too good when the day started, was not a bit improved by the experience. Even rich nations can feel like paupers. That's how the country felt that night.

Neither the nation's 31-million individual shareholders, nor the more numerous millions whose financial fates were bound up in pension funds, insurance, and profit-sharing plans, would have been heartened had they known that worse, quite a lot worse, was to come, and quickly. The storm did not abate overnight.

The same people who got up and went to work on Wall Street on Monday the 25th, also got up and went to work on

* One of the longest-standing proposals in a place famed for its long-standing (and unenacted) proposals calls for the conversion of quotations of prices into decimals. The change would be eminently sensible. I never expect to see it.

Tuesday the 26th, but it was not very long before they were all wondering why they had gone through the struggle to get to that overbuilt, overpopulated, yet still desolate region in the first place. People who commute to Wall Street, and that includes just about everybody who works there, are a pretty hardy breed, and they seem to be able to survive just about anything. Still, that Tuesday tested their mettle with an acid as corrosive as any that had been spilled since 1929. In 30 minutes after the opening gong sounded on that rainy Tuesday, the Dow Jones Industrial Averages sank another four points. Then, for about three hours, there ensued one of those inexplicable and curious instances of financial history, which will forever put complicating little jiggles—mute but eloquent—in the lines that trace the day's happenings. The averages, in short, started to move up. No news warranted that rise, no clear cause explained it, and while people were still trying to arrive at a rationale for the rally, it ended. During the brief, bright flight of that Roman candle, the four points lost in the first 30 minutes were made up, and there was actually a gain of 3 1/2 points more.

But around the time that Wall Street has its sandwich, the market ran out of steam. Prices again began to rush downhill. The Dow was off seven points by 2:00 P.M., and at the close it was off 10.20 points, to another new closing low for the year, 631.16. The Dow, at one point, touched 627.46 before turning up slightly.

Those tough-minded men, the optimists—not just the ones on the Street but the ones that reside elsewhere as well—like to say that "once you hit bottom, there is no place to go but up." This has always seemed to me a highly disputable statement, there being no logical reason why you could not hit bottom and just stay there. However, on this occasion, on the sunny morning of May 27 that followed a week of fog and drizzle, I found myself in agreement with the optimists. The market was going to move. Up did seem to be the only direction for it to take.

And up it turned out to go. At the gong, the first trade that crossed the ticker was a routine 400 shares of Talley Industries preferred at 11 7/8—a price unchanged from the previous day's close. But the next trade, 500 shares of Kroger, sold at 25—up 3/8, or more understandably, up 37½ ¢ per share, a total increase in value for the 500-share lot of $187.50. Virtually every other trade on that Wednesday followed the initial upward pattern. The ticker chattered on and on, with each trade revealing prices higher than the previous quotes. The Dow Jones Average at 11:00 A.M. was up 13.62 points; at noon, 18.28 points; at 1:00 P.M., 20.67 points; at 2:00 P.M., 21.09; and at the close, up a smashing 32.04. Thus, in a day in which 17,460,000 shares were traded—the second most active day of the year until then—all of the two previous days' losses, in terms of the averages anyway, were made up. May 27 also achieved the distinction, which it held until August 16, 1971—the day after President Nixon's historic announcement freezing wages and prices, and suspending the obligation of the U.S. Treasury to redeem dollars with gold— of recording the largest single gain in the history of the Dow Jones Industrial Averages. The averages have been computed since 1896. The largest gain previously recorded was on November 26, 1963, when, in another conspicuous rebound, the index had gone up 32.03 points. The momentous event then was the three-day funeral of President Kennedy, which had ended the day before.

There were lots of people around Merrill Lynch, myself included, who expected stocks to go up on May 27, or very soon thereafter, following the sharp slides of Monday and Tuesday. But no one, and I shall have to include myself and most of my colleagues in this judgment, expected a rise so swift and so broadly based. Most professionals, I believe, were looking for a modest upward thrust as a result of technical action, rather than an historic advance spurred by deeper causes.

The Dow Jones was not the only index to show improvement that day. The New York Stock Exchange's own index (G) of all common stocks listed on the Exchange, which is a weighted average of some 1,400 stocks, showed a gain of 1.96 points. *The New York Times,* which as part of its general stance of being special in all things also has its own average (G), reported its average up 19.15 points. Standard & Poor's index (G) of 500 representative stocks listed on the New York Exchange was up 3.48 points. The American Stock Exchange, which had been plagued with low volume throughout the year and whose stocks had been listless or worse, had its best day in eight years. Volume on the Amex rose to 5,887,105 shares, its best trading day of 1970.

As with the decline, the rise showed some remarkable performances among individual stocks. Some idea of the extent of this seesaw movement among the averages and among some 50 leading stocks is conveyed in the table on page 22.

No doubt, many people in the world can look at that table

Swingers of the Week
WEEK OF MAY 25–29, 1970

	May 25 Low	Week's Low	Week's High	Percentage Increase (low to high)
Dow Jones Industrial Average (intra-day highs and lows)	639.10	627.46	703.86	12.2
Sears	53 1/8	51	57 7/8	13.5
General Telephone	21	20 3/4	25 1/8	21.4
Memorex	64 1/8	64 1/8	76 5/8	19.3
Avon Products	131 1/2	128 1/2	150	16.7
Burroughs Corp.	100 3/8	100 1/8	122 3/8	22.2
Coca-Cola	63 5/8	63	71 3/8	13.3
Walt Disney Productions	102	96 1/2	118	22.3
Eastman Kodak	60 1/4	57 5/8	63 1/2	10.2
Holiday Inns	22	19 3/4	26 1/2	34.2
IBM	241	238	279 3/4	17.5
Procter & Gamble	41 1/2	40 1/8	49 3/4	24.0
Xerox Corp.	72 3/8	70	82 1/2	17.9
R. J. Reynolds	35 1/8	34 3/8	39	13.5
Zenith Radio	22 1/2	22 1/4	26 7/8	20.8

and be totally unmoved by what they see. I also have no doubt that it is a very good thing that so many people, perhaps the majority, can read such figures without emotion. Varied talents are stirred by varied stimuli—also a good thing. But as far as Wall Street is concerned, those figures are very dramatic and very eloquent. No good financial man could look at numbers like those and remain uninterested. To us, they spell history—loud and clear.

People who watch market prices on Wall Street are somewhat like baseball fans. And, like baseball, Wall Street's business—what has been called "the money game"—is one of the most carefully observed activities in the world. Statistics abound in infinite variety. History is carefully recorded, and its precedent is constantly being cited to prove points, win arguments or explain away what Wall Street fears more than anything else—the unknown.

The previous stock market break that most resembled what happened in May of 1970 had come eight years before—uncannily enough, eight years to the very week. On May 28, 1962, the Dow Jones Average of industrials dropped 34.95 points, the greatest fall in a single day in history except

Gross National Product
Seasonally Adjusted Annual Rate

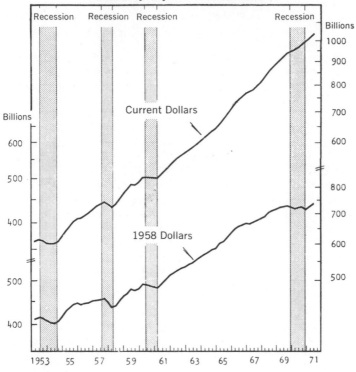

SOURCE: Department of Commerce.

for October 28, 1929, when the drop was 38.33 points. Volume on May 28, 1962, was the fifth largest in history up to that point: 9,350,000 shares. On Tuesday, May 29, 1962, stocks continued to slide rapidly to levels far below Monday's close, but only in the morning; around noon, the market changed direction, and the Dow Jones ended up 27.03 points higher than it had closed the day before. The markets were closed on Wednesday, May 30, which was Memorial Day. Then, on Thursday, May 31, 1962, on volume of almost 11-million shares, the Dow Jones gained 9.40 more, and ended up the day slightly ahead of the Monday opening. John Brooks, a writer with considerable acumen about Wall Street, remarked that "the crisis ran its course in three days, but, needless to say, the postmortem took longer." It always does.

The postmortems in 1962, like those that followed the days in May 1970, inevitably involved the usual delve into the record books to find historical parallels. At that time, the best precedent that anyone could come up with was October 1929. But the atmosphere was so different in 1929—the internal economic and financial conditions, and indeed the entire domestic and international situations, were so unlike those of 1962—that the search for historical comparisons did not lead to any very significant conclusion. History could not teach us much.

The search for parallels in 1970, inevitably, led back to 1962. But again the similarities were only superficial. In 1962 the stock market's sudden slump and recovery came in the midst of a good economic year (see chart on page 23). By contrast, 1970 was a year of borderline recession. In 1962 the great unexpected force striking from outside was the sudden, and to some degree ill-tempered, move by President Kennedy against the steel companies, which had just imposed sizable across-the-board price increases. In 1970 the market was not responding to a single swift force, but rather to the accumulating weight of depressing events.

In the crisis of May 1962, the mutual funds played a role quite different from the one they played in May 1970. In 1962 the funds were heavy buyers on the Monday that stock prices were coming down, and they were heavy sellers on the Thursday that the market was rebounding. Thus, they acted as stabilizers in a fluctuating market. Not so, as we shall see, in 1970.

One of Wall Street's seers told John Brooks following the 1962 affair: "As to whether what happened can happen again —of course it can. I think that people may be more careful for a year or two, and then we may see another speculative buildup followed by another crash, and so on until God makes people less greedy." The seer was, in fact, seeing quite clearly at that particular moment, as the events of May 1970 testified. (But, as though to prove history never repeats exactly, we also had a spring rally in 1971, and a series of surges and retreats following the President's actions on August 15, 1971. The market finished strong in 1971.)

So, as with the resemblances between 1962 and 1929, the resemblances between 1962 and 1970 are, after all, superficial. They don't teach us much except to reinforce the generalities that outside forces have effects and that markets can be volatile—and that we knew already.

In a public speech I made a couple of years ago, I told the story of the man who went to see his doctor and was told he was paranoiac. "That may be true," the man said, "but that does not keep my friends from plotting against me." The point of the story is that Wall Street sometimes does appear to be a hatching ground for plots. We do not usually have trials, and we never shoot defeated plotters. But the Street is very much given over to detailed and sometimes agonizing self-scrutiny. During these days the analysis was particularly intense. Everybody was asking: What happened? How did it happen? Why did it happen? And, of course, will it happen again?

To answer those questions, we have to go back a bit in time.

CHAPTER II

Some Reasons Why

IN LOOKING FOR THE ANSWER TO THOSE questions, a good starting point is 1968—just before the inauguration, but after the election, of President Nixon. In that winter, there was a brief springtime of national hope. The business community, in particular, had good reason for optimism. After all, the first Republican Administration since 1960 was coming to power. In June 1968, the Republican party was still assumed to be very much the party of business. More nuances and refinements of that assumption than anyone foresaw have emerged since; but, in 1968, the correlation of interests seemed unquestioned. The prediction was that the fiscal irresponsibility of the outgoing Democratic regime would soon be ended. Hopes were high that somehow a settlement of the sad and prolonged war in Vietnam would soon be reached.

The belief that the Government would soon formulate and enforce conservative fiscal and prudent monetary policies was central to the confidence of business. Only in that way could sound progress in the national economy be achieved. Excessive spending by the Government and excessive increases in the available supply of money (G) over the past couple of years, especially in 1968, had spelled inflation—at an ever-increasing velocity. Inflation is the worst enemy of prosperity. To check it would make sound growth once again possible—so ran the rationale.

But by May of 1970 many of those happy omens had changed. Neither the domestic nor the foreign situation appeared to the public at large to have improved very much. Cynicism had replaced high hope. The national spirit was once again depressed. The level of politics was uninspired.

In economic terms, the principal reasons for the reversal

26

were not hard to find. For months there had been very little increase in the money supply, said to be the pump of inflation —but the inflation rate had continued its stubborn upward course. Unemployment was going up stubbornly, too. At that time, inflation was running at the annual rate of 6%, which, as it turned out, was about its high point. The unemployment rate had gone up to 5%—an increase in the number of unemployed of about 1,085,000 persons over a year earlier. And it had further yet to go.

So evidence was gathering that the efforts to control inflation were not succeeding. The dominant fear was that the only way they could succeed would be to prolong them until the nation was plunged into a deep recession. In conversation and in journalism, discussion of the current economic situation was peppered with references to 1929. As with the other citations of the past that we have discussed, most of the references were in terms of parallels, rather than predictions. But all of them were disturbing nonetheless as measures of the depths of the prevalent pessimism.

Now, Wall Street is a great place for stories—outside of prisons, the greatest. At this juncture, the story that comes to my mind concerns W. C. Fields, who was once discovered by a friend to be reading the Holy Scriptures. Surprised, the friend asked what was going on. Fields replied: "I am looking for loopholes." Any discussion about the economic mood of the nation should always leave plenty of loopholes, and of generous diameter, since generalities about mood obviously are after all only generalities. People do not act in accordance with the best forecasts, or even in accordance with the dictates of their own intelligence, at all times.

The point is that the rather grim economic outlook in May need not have had the consequence that took place in the markets of May. Indeed, the economic outlook in May was not very different from what it had been in April—so that one cannot explain May 25 simply by pointing to this rather glum and listless atmosphere. One must go deeper.

The real explanation lies in a confluence of several elements, of which economics was only one. We do not live in an economic, but rather in a political-economic world. Non-economic factors can have startling economic results. A series of political, psychological and foreign events, apparently running on different tracks, finally collided in May. More than the climate, they explain the bad days.

The invasion of Cambodia was launched on April 29. To

that new military intervention the nation's articulate youth reacted far more vigorously than the Administration had anticipated. A depressing sense that the war in southeast Asia would never end was spreading, and indeed the quick consensus, later considerably revised, was that this strike constituted a further enlargement of the war, whose outcome could not be predicted. Demonstrations on the nation's campuses were bordering on the violent, and then turned both violent and tragic with the killings at Kent State University—a further depressant to the national spirit. It was a curiosity of history that a tragedy on the campus of a university in Ohio somehow linked to zero growth in the money supply and to a squeeze of corporate liquidity and to growing fears of a money panic—but such a strange linkage did take place.

At certain times one of the most reliable barometers of the nation's mood is Wall Street itself. At this time Wall Street was becoming mired in its own as well as in the national trouble. Not only were markets dull, trading low, and investors passive, but some Wall Street firms themselves were beginning to teeter. The biggest news of the year, viewed from the Street, was shaping up.

To make matters worse, no one in Washington seemed even to be watching the barometer. A few weeks before the first of the three climactic days of May—by coincidence, on April 29, the opening date of the Cambodian invasion—a group of Wall Streeters, of which I was one, met at the White House with the President's leading economic advisers and their assistants to discuss the condition of the Street. The tone of the meeting was dejected. It generally took the direction of an appraisal of the effects on the stock market if some brokerage firms, weakened by low volume and by the ensuing decline in their revenues, were to fail. Little affirmative action was proposed or taken, although the current White House strategy was reviewed. Insufficient attention was given to the true importance of the Street to the nation, and to the real message and meaning of the market, which I summed up publicly in this way: "The economy lies at the heart of the nation, and Wall Street lies at the heart of the economy." That message was not to be heard or understood for yet a month or more.

Bad news feeds on itself. All of these troublesome developments both within and outside of the economic arena began to engage the minds and dictate the responses of the large institutional investors—those guardians and trustees of more than $150-billion of other people's money. Surveying the scene, these people, who buy and sell huge blocks of stock, determined that it was a bad time to buy stock. By so determining, they tended to confirm their own forecasts.

In brief, they moved to what we call a cash position—putting or keeping in cash somewhere between 8% and 15% of the total of the vast funds under their control. Obviously, that meant fewer buyers and still more sellers, and became one of the causal factors bringing on the incredibly rapid slippage that I have described. Plenty of slippage, of course, had already occurred. From December of 1969 to the middle of May of 1970 the loss in market value of all listed and unlisted securities was enormous: roughly $280-billion. The drop of May 25 and 26 came on top of that decline. We were very close to panic in the Street, and in the streets as well.

As I've said, the big institutional investors can sometimes make their decisions sound ones by the mere fact of making them. In a roughly similar way, a falling market can accelerate its rate of fall—for example, by means of its direct and serious effect on people who buy stocks on margin (**G**).

With falling prices, lots of firms found themselves obliged to put out margin calls (**G**) to their customers. A customer receives a margin call—a call for additional funds—when the equity in the securities that he owns has dropped below the permissible limits of margin. The call is a demand for additional capital. The customer must respond in one simple but very eloquent way: he has to put up more money or securities to protect his investment. If he is unable to do so, then enough of his securities must be liquidated to raise the needed amount. It is well to understand in this connection, by the way, that the brokerage firm has no option in such matters. The Federal Reserve Board sets the margin requirements (**G**), which it reduced from 80% to 65% in May 1970. The margin requirements were further reduced to 55% in December 1971. Brokerage firms are obliged by the rules of various stock exchanges to call on the customer for equity when margin limits (**G**) are exceeded.

Some statistics from Merrill Lynch make an interesting illustration of the effects of margin buying in a declining market. On the last day of February 1970—three months before the period we are now discussing—the daily margin calls issued by Merrill Lynch totaled $1.6-million. At the end of March, with the market slightly better, the daily calls totaled $1.4-million. But the April downturn that started so abruptly forced margin calls upward. On April 24 margin calls totaled $6.3-

million—almost four times their total at the end of February. On May 20, which was a slow and sliding day but not one marked by a sharp drop in prices, margin calls came to $9.3-million. On May 22, a Friday, they totaled $11.5-million. It seems a sound assumption that much of the sudden selling that developed on May 25 and May 26 was caused by the fact that margin buyers had run out of cash or securities to pledge to protect their loans, and were either forced to or chose to liquidate their holdings. Thus, the number of sellers multiplied. Those sales push down the price of the stock being sold, and as a consequence there may be further margin calls. The response of prices could only be to move further down.

Besides margin sellers, what the Street calls short sales (**G**) were also very much in evidence. At this particular juncture, the short sellers decided that the stocks were going to continue to go down. They sold borrowed stock with the hope of buying it back at lower prices. That had a further depressing effect.

Of course other aspects of the business scene were very much affected by this visible and highly publicized crisis of the stock markets. Corporations often depend for their financing on their ability to sell stock on the open market. But they are reluctant to sell part of their company at what appears at the time to be a very cheap price. At the depressed levels of May 1970, very few corporations judged the moment propitious to raise additional capital from the equity markets. A few examples make the point: Memorex was down from 163 in 1967 to around 60; Getty Oil, which had been well over 100 in 1967, was down to around 40. So the managers of corporate finance decided not to raise additional capital by selling stock at that time. Accordingly, they were cash poor—and "poor" was becoming a pretty common adjective.

Mergers also slowed down. Again, the reason was the decline in value of the securities of the corporations contemplating merger. Many corporations are willing to merge if they can exchange their stock for another company's stock of higher price or higher potential. But corporations that were willing to exchange their stock at $70 to $80 a share during 1968 or 1969 were naturally very reluctant to trade their shares at a price of $20 in 1970's spring. And many stocks in the $70-to-$80 range were down to the $20-level at this time. Their prices in relation to earnings were also dropping. That meant more inertia—more lack of action—in securities markets and in the business community in general. No action means bad business.

Hardest hit were the conglomerates, for which mergers had been almost a way of life. The table below shows the precipitous price declines some conglomerates experienced in the two years from the spring of 1968 to the spring of 1970.

Prices of a Representative Group of Conglomerates

Company	(April 15, 1968) Price	(April 15, 1970) Price	Percent Decline
City Investing	$ 21.93	$17.50	20.2%
Gulf & Western	41.50	15.13	63.6
Walter Kidde	66.15	35.75	46.0
Leasco Data Processing	28.80	14.00	51.4
Ling-Temco-Vought	115.88	18.13	84.4
Teledyne	55.67	20.13	63.9
Average for group			53.8%

(Prices adjusted for stock splits and stock dividends.)

Ling-Temco-Vought's case is especially interesting. At its zenith LTV was the majority owner of 11 companies, including such well known firms as Jones & Laughlin, Wilson & Co., LTV Aerospace and Braniff Airways. In the lush markets of the mid-1960s the stock zoomed to ever higher altitudes, reaching a peak of $169.50 on August 7, 1967. But when the stock market began to turn around, LTV had to sell off some of its very substantial interests to avert the threat of bankruptcy. With its stock plummeting, LTV could no longer use the leverage of its once high-flying shares to acquire new companies that would generate the earnings required to service its heavy debts.

LTV's interests in three of the companies, Okonite, Wilson Sporting Goods and Wilson Pharmaceutical, were sold directly to other firms. Its interest in the three other firms that it disposed of, Braniff, Computer Technology and National Car Rental, were sold in stages. While these major parts of LTV's untidy empire were being spun off, its stock dropped steadily downward, hitting a low of 7 1/8 on that black Monday, May

25, 1970. At that price LTV was worth less than 5% of the price it reached at its all-time high in August 1967. The chart on page 33 shows LTV's divestitures and the concurrent rapid decline of its stock.

Along with the depressing effect of the declining stock market, then, went other depressants in many other areas. In fact, the drop in values of the market made a kind of concentrate, which penetrated to a thousand other sectors related to American business. The most popular story making the rounds at this time of sorrow concerns two brokers who were walking down the street talking about market conditions.

> ONE BROKER TO THE OTHER: How are you bearing up under all of this? Can you sleep nights?
> SECOND BROKER: Sure, I sleep like a baby.
> FIRST BROKER: What do you mean, you sleep like a baby?
> SECOND BROKER: I wake up every three hours and cry.

A second story just as popular had the same two characters in a bar around the corner from the Stock Exchange.

> FIRST BROKER: In March my dog was run over, my house burned down, and I broke my leg.
> SECOND BROKER: In March, the bottom dropped out of mutual funds.
> FIRST BROKER: In April, my daughter ran away with a man who has no job, I wrecked my car, and on top of that I took a huge pay cut.
> SECOND BROKER: In April, General Motors and LTV went to hell, and I lost $100,000.
> FIRST BROKER: In May, my wife left me for another man. What could be worse than that?
> SECOND BROKER: June.

Through all of that figurative rain, even what little good news there was turned out to be hard to perceive. One news item aroused very little interest and, indeed, only a few cynical remarks when it appeared on the Dow Jones ticker. Later it turned out to be an event of great importance and a kind of pivotal point in the history of those days. The news came on Monday afternoon from the White House, in the form of an announcement that President Nixon had invited to dinner on that Wednesday night some 60 to 100 leading figures from the business and financial communities. I was among those invited.

I'll describe the dinner in detail in a later chapter. In this context, the significance comes with the simple fact of the

LTV'S Divestitures and Exchanges

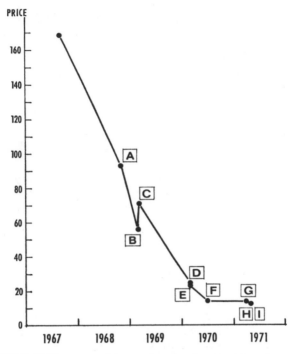

A 10/31/68: LTV announced terms of previously proposed exchange offer of LTV warrants and stock in National Car, Braniff, and Computer Technology for LTV common shares and debentures.

B 2/17/69: LTV announced plans to sell remaining interest in National Car. Sale made to Household Finance.

C 2/25/69: LTV sold part of Braniff stock via public offering.

D 2/19/70: LTV said it would sell its interests in Braniff and Okonite in order to retain controlling interest in Jones & Laughlin.

E 2/24/70: LTV announced terms of sale of Wilson Sporting Goods to Pepsi-Co.

F 6/5/70: LTV announced agreements to sell 75% interest in Wilson Pharmaceutical to American Can.

G 3/16/71: LTV announced program aimed at divesting Braniff. Part to be accomplished by stock offering (completed) and part by exchange offer.

H 4/2/71: Wilson & Company proposal to buy 1,150,000 common shares from LTV approved by Wilson directors. On 4/6/71 approved by LTV directors.

I 4/2/71: Filed registration statement to exchange combination of Braniff Airways and LTV stock for the 5% debentures.

announcement. The topics that were to be discussed, according to press rumor, included the state of the economy and the financial markets, and the progress of the incursion into Cambodia. Ever since the beginning of the Cambodian maneuvers, as we've seen, the market had been going down. Properly or not, analysts and brokers were establishing a causal relationship here: that is, they were contending that Cambodia was contributing to the bearish attitude of the investor.

This may seem a paradox, in view of the old maxim about war and Wall Street. But the fact is that there is in truth no paradox: war is bad news, and this one was particularly bad news at that time. The bad news was only slightly alleviated by a comment from Secretary of Defense Melvin Laird to the effect that the schedule announced by the Administration for the withdrawal of American troops from Vietnam was going to be met or beaten; that the thrust into Cambodia was militarily very successful; and that it would be followed by prompt withdrawal of American troops from that area, also on schedule. Most of these estimates, despite their validity, were, in the language of the Street, discounted.

By Tuesday night, however, the White House announcement of the dinner to be held the following night was beginning to attract more attention. The coming event was discussed and speculated about on the television news on Tuesday night; it was featured prominently in Eastern newspapers on Wednesday morning. Thus, although the first announcement had passed with only a ripple on Monday, awareness of it was now spreading in waves. Its possible importance gradually came to be understood. Investors, large and small, had a chance to reflect on the significance of this meeting. *The New York Times* remarked that "at long last the Administration is beginning to realize the seriousness of the decline in the stock and bond markets." Further, while Laird's pledges had been discussed lightly the day before, they were presently given new credence in the public mind when coupled with the White House meeting. The whole began to equal something more than the sum of the parts. And the stage was set for the dramatic market rise discussed in Chapter I.

On Thursday, May 28, the day following the dinner, encouraging reports of what had taken place began to seep out. The averages, as we've noted, had bounded back dramatically on the day before. Now the market continued its upward thrust. The performance on Thursday was not as strong, nor as broad, as the advance of the previous day, but it was still very encouraging. Volume rose to 18,910,000 shares on the New York Stock Exchange, then the record for 1970, and also the highest volume since December 31, 1969, when 19,380,000 shares changed hands. On May 28, 1,211 issues advanced while only 271 retreated. The market opened with a tremendous rush to buy. Part of the rush came from formerly skittish foreign investors, who had decided that the time had arrived to step into the United States market once more. In the first hour of trading the Dow Jones Industrial Average was up 18.41 points, a nigh unbelievable move following Wednesday's rise. Volume in the first hour was 5,650,000 shares—the heaviest first-hour volume since October 22, 1969.

As usual in such a market, after the quick advance, profit-taking ensued. The market dipped for the next two hours, and then, starting in the afternoon, the market took a long breath and pushed upward again. The Dow Jones ended the day up 20.95 points, another big advance. The total gain for the two days was a startling 52.99 points, a record for two days. Institutional trading on that Thursday was much larger than it had been the day before. Eighty-five blocks of 10,000 shares or more, representing a total value of $41,610,451, changed hands.

The covering of short positions was certainly a reason for much of the buying that occurred on Thursday. In such a rally this is almost always the case. While short selling can bring on quick declines, it can also paradoxically help the market to rally, since one effect of short covering is to put a floor under market prices.

The mutual funds, while they were maintaining large cash positions, were also looking for bargains, particularly among the blue chip stocks. Hence the sharp increase among blue chips and such leading glamour issues as IBM, Disney, Burroughs, and Avon Products (see table Chapter I, p. 22).

Even with that kind of rise, however, every stock did not go up—buttressing the age-old and absolutely sound argument that the investor must always be selective. Telex, the second most active stock, slipped 1/8 of a point (a decline of 12½ cents). Texas Instruments lost one. In an ominous note, heard by all too few, Penn Central, fourth on the most active list, dropped 1/8 to 13 1/4. The railroad's management had announced that a subsidiary had postponed a $100-million offering of debentures because the company feared that the issue would encounter difficulties when it reached the market. That fear was especially significant in light of the fact that borrowers then were willing to pay a near-record 10½% interest for money.

On balance, though, despite these particulars, the trend was up. And the New York Stock Exchange's membership was not the only beneficiary of this new spirit and new evidence of buyers' interest. On the American Stock Exchange, Wednesday's rise continued into Thursday. The American Exchange had its heaviest trading session of the year, with volume hitting 6,819,240 shares.

Non-business reasons, or at least reasons that were only very indirectly related to business, once again played an important role in charting the market's course that day. The White House dinner was only one of these. The word was circulating that the session at the White House the night before had been amiable, that the President had shown a real understanding of the importance of stock prices to the national economy, that he had also displayed a general sympathy with the problems of the business community and that somehow he was going to "do something." As I'll relate later, I can testify that such reports were generally soundly based.

Also gaining currency were some remarks reported to have been made at the dinner by Arthur Burns, Chairman of the Federal Reserve Board, to the effect that "I did not become Chairman of the Federal Reserve Board to add to the problem of inflation," and that "I am keenly aware of the continuing danger of inflation." Once again, I can vouch for the fact that he did indeed make these remarks. Since the market's early tremors, and indeed the long dull months of bear market from 1969 onwards were mostly caused by the spiraling inflation rate, these assurances of Burns' meant a good deal. They had a salutary effect. (They also helped to explode another myth: the stock market does not fatten on inflation.)

In the marketplace, Friday saw more of Thursday's kind of rally. The stock market continued its advance. The morning session was dull compared with those that had preceded it. But around 2:00 P.M. the averages, which at that time were 7.05 above their opening levels, began to spurt. By 3 P.M. the averages had more than doubled their earlier advance, to a total of 14.44 points. At the close the averages were up 16.29 for the day.

With that gain, the Dow Jones Industrial Average had pierced the 700 level to 700.44. *The New York Times* index was up 9.30 points. While volume was down somewhat to 14.63-million shares, the volume for the week of 80,680,697 shares represented one of the most active weeks in the history of the Exchange. The week before, volume had been only 59.6-million shares. Indeed, it turned out to be Wall Street's busiest week since October 13, 1969, when 82.5-million shares changed hands. Since then, the week of February 1, 1971, when 105,711,500 shares were traded, has set the new record for Wall Street's busiest week. The week of August 16, 1971—following the imposition of the wage-price freeze and other economic actions by the President—failed to break this record by some 420,000 shares, despite the fact that August 16 still stands as the Exchange's biggest single day.

The over-the-counter market did equally well. It reacted in tandem with the New York and the American exchanges. Prices on the over-the-counter market dropped the first two days of the week, then rallied on Wednesday and extended the rallies on Thursday and Friday. Eli Lilly, a blue chip that was traded over the counter, rose $5.50 a share. Anheuser-Busch was up $8 from its low asking price. Banking and insurance stocks generally advanced. A selection of a few of the good quality over-the-counter stocks, and a record of their performance that week, follows.

Some OTC Stocks and Their Bid Range during Week of May 25–29, 1970

	Week's Low Bid	Week's High Bid
Barnes Hind Pharmaceutical	34 1/4	38
Brush Beryllium	13 5/8	17 3/8
A. C. Nielson, Class A common	27	31
Raychem	75	88
O. M. Scott	16	19 1/2
Tampax	147	160
Tecumseh Products	98	105

How can this dramatic turn-around on all the equity markets be explained?

Looking back, it is impossible to give a precise explanation of what had happened, attributing an exact amount of the decline to this or that event and assigning proportionate weight to the various elements of the recovery. Among other things, the stock market is a mood, and moods can never be fully explained.

Still, my own analysis assigns a vital role in the recovery to the individual investor. I believe the individual investor in the United States suddenly found that he did not really accept and give credence to all the predictions of gloom and doom that were filling the air. The independent individual looked around him and came to an independent conclusion. He decided that the country wasn't going to hell in a handbasket. He determined that the Administration was, after all, interested in and concerned about the future of business and the business community. He concluded that the management of the economy at that moment was not, in fact, being hopelessly bungled. He put some faith in the efficacy of what was then called "the game plan," the government's program for managing the economy. As it later turned out, the game plan had to be dramatically changed, partly because of the force of *political* economics—but remember this is May 1970, and certain indicators were pointing up the long-range soundness of the plan.

So he buried his skepticism about the future of the economy. He also reasoned that the hysteria evoked by the Cambodian invasion was overdone. To him, at least at that moment, Cambodia did not look like such a disastrous mistake. The South Vietnamese army seemed to be acquitting itself quite well, and the possibilities of success for "Vietnamization" seemed fairly good. Certainly the individual investor must have thought that the process of Vietnamization was succeeding better than most commentators were telling him.

As for business conditions, corporations of course had cash shortages. But irresponsible predictions of a liquidity panic were properly dismissed by the individual investor, out of faith if not out of knowledge. Both the Fed and the White House were pledged not to permit such a crisis, and they seemed to have the ability to avert it. In short, the fearsome forecasts that had made for speculative excesses on the downside seemed vastly exaggerated.

On a more practical level, a historic buying opportunity was presenting itself. Whether by instinct, good advice, or good analysis, thousands of individual investors, particularly those between the coasts, saw bargains and decided to pick them up. I am tempted to conclude, perhaps in part because I want to do so, that the calm, stiff-backboned individual American investor rescued other members of the investing public, including the professionals, from their own folly.

By Friday, May 29, everybody who was interested, and that meant just about everybody in the country, knew that he had lived through a memorable week. Journalists, many of whom tend to be bored by Wall Street and often overlook the true importance of events taking place there, focused on the Street as the big story of the week. *Newsweek* magazine, which I should add has an excellent business section and is not among the journals that neglect finance, termed the week of May 25 "the stock market's wildest week." *Newsweek* suggested that the longest bear market since the Great Depression had finally turned around. At the very least, said *Newsweek,* "the despair that had gripped Wall Street and the business community for weeks seems to have been decisively shattered; in its place was the tentative and still fragile mood of muted hope." *Newsweek* added: "Most of the nation's investors had been holding on precariously in the rage of a deep bear market . . . in a curious way the week's eye-popping rally was a vindication of stubborn bullishness—a triumph of amateurs who were betting against the pessimism of the hard-bitten pros . . . a vindication for Mr. Nixon himself."

Indeed, as we have seen, the amateurs acquired new fame and new respect by their performance during that week in May. At Merrill Lynch, we knew where the individual was and what he was doing because we study his movements very closely through our 200 branch offices around the country. Generally, we know that the individual investor has a strong tendency to buy and hold stocks, rather than to buy and trade them. That tendency became much more pronounced in this period in May. At this time the reports coming in from our offices clearly supported the view that "heartland America" was doing most of the buying. It was clear to us that people in Middle America—in places like Little Rock and Houston and Albuquerque—were moving into the market in strength. At the same time, the amount of brokerage done by our offices in the big seaboard cities was falling off.

So, not only were individuals supplying the strength, but they were evidently individuals who at the time were being described as "the silent majority" (a phrase that has already disappeared from our political lexicon). The Administration had insisted all along that the bear market's gloom was being generated by financial leaders of the northeastern states, who were unduly affected by the antiwar environment in which they lived. The record of those days supports that argument. Of course, Mr. Nixon, properly enough, was doing everything he could to enlist the help of the financial establishment, particularly at that Wednesday dinner. But the real stock buyers were not the pros but the investing public—perhaps a new group, a kind of "financial silent majority," which had not acted in concert before.

The New York Times, for all of its identification with the people in those northeastern states, almost always recognizes a good story. The *Times* assigned one of its top financial reporters, Eileen Shanahan, to analyze just what had happened on Wall Street during the week that was. Her conclusions were that "well-to-do individuals—those who generally buy stocks in 100-share round lots—appear to have been responsible for halting the great stock slide of April and May." Mutual funds, banks and insurance companies, whose activities helped to trigger the downturn, were still sitting on the sidelines.

In her article, Miss Shanahan correctly quoted me as saying that "Merrill Lynch's records disclosed striking differences in the investment patterns of its customers in different parts of the country. Heartland America was buying all the way down." While Merrill Lynch's offices in the central part of the country showed no declines in buy orders, those offices on the coasts from Boston to Miami in the East to San Francisco and Los Angeles in the West, emphatically including New York City, saw a drying up of buy orders from mid-April on. When the turnaround came in the last week in May, I am also accurately quoted as saying, "it was because the round lot buyers on both coasts—not the little Aunt Janes who buy a few shares at a time, but business executives and professional men—came back into the market. They did so apparently simply because they thought the price declines had reached the point where stocks were a good buy."

Miss Shanahan also talked at length to Stan West, the director of research for the New York Stock Exchange. He told her that "with the volume running from 14- to 16-million shares changing hands most days" he would have expected to see 100 or more big blocks traded. That was the pattern set during the upturn of the market in the past. But in this particular rally, the numbers of big blocks ran around 70—relatively quite a low figure. Mr. West's figures gave further support to our conviction at Merrill Lynch that although institutions were net buyers of stock in April, they were net sellers in May.

Until that time, some question remained whether individual

investors could really turn around the market, since institutions then accounted for some 56% of the daily trading on
the New York Stock Exchange. But the answer to the question seems to be a resounding yes. If only 130,000 individual
investors, or less than one-half of 1% of the total of 31-
million individual stockholders in the United States, decided
to each buy one round lot of 100 shares, they could make a
13-million share day all by themselves. And, of course, if
they were all potential buyers on any given day, they would
force prices upward. The individual can still influence the
market's movements. He can and always will find a place in
the market. Institutions do not and will not own the marketplace.

While the experiences of May restored the faith of individual investors, May's events badly shook another faith—
obviously, one less well-based. For all of the flackery, the
fact remains that institutional buyers, alleged to be stabilizers
in the market and generally pretty cool customers making
emotionless decisions, were just as susceptible to panic, if
not more so, as anyone else. They sold on the way down and
waited until after the upturn before they started buying again.
It may not be fair to say that they have "feet of clay," but to
say at least that they have feet—in other words that they are
human, and vulnerable to emotional responses—is clear
enough. The market is people, after all.

CHAPTER III

The Economy
Behind It All

THE ANSWERS TO HOW IT ALL HAPPENED, AND
why it all happened, as I have indicated, can never be precise.
But the very imprecision is what makes the game of analysis
so intriguing. The appeal of the game is apparent from the
number of people who play it. Everybody cares. Many prac-
titioners of the game, not only on Wall Street but all over the
world, expend lots of time and energy and an ocean of words
trying to analyze the stock market. In newspapers, magazines,
private conversations, around the bar or over the dinner table,
the urge to talk about the market is very strong. I can testify
that it is rarely resisted.

According to the latest statistics based on a recent study by
the New York Stock Exchange, one out of every four American
adults owns stock. Three out of every four are affected in some
material way by the course of the stock market. I daresay the
fourth is not immune, either, although the effect on him of a
bull market or a bear must be presumed to be less direct.

Such high numbers are not hard to explain. Everybody who
owns an insurance policy has a personal interest in the market
because the insurance companies invest a portion of their reserves, built up through the payment of premiums, in stocks
and bonds. Very important purchasers of common stocks in
the last few years have been the pension funds—with the
result that everyone on a pension, or with the prospects of one,
can see his future in the rise and fall of those lines on the
charts. Colleges and universities, which hold the key to so
many important developments in the present and future of
our society, invest their endowment more and more in common stocks. Once they put it into nothing more venturesome
than Government bonds. Some leading universities may now

42

have 70% of their money committed to common stocks. The University of Rochester and Wesleyan University are notable examples: they have large holdings in the Xerox Corporation, whose Business Products Group is located in Rochester. Even the most hard-bitten trustee would have trouble finding fault with that investment over the years.

During the great bull market of 1967 and 1968, McGeorge Bundy, now head of the Ford Foundation and Special Assistant to the President for National Security Affairs in both the Kennedy and Johnson administrations, urged universities and colleges to invest in the stock market to increase their yields. The implication was that the trustees had an obligation to do this in order to get the best results from their capital and to lessen the demand for money from outside sources—among them the Ford Foundation. This is indisputably good advice while the stock market is going up. It is less good when it is coming down.

The case of the Penn Central supplies an ironic footnote to the proclivity for common stock investment. Several of the directors of Penn Central were also trustees of their alma mater, the University of Pennsylvania. After the Penn Central was driven into reorganization under Section 77 of the Bankruptcy Act in June of 1970, there came to light the fact that the University of Pennsylvania had lost $3.5-million on its investment in Penn Central.* In 1971, it now develops, many other institutions may have lost much larger sums, which could total hundreds of millions. The wisest of men do not know what the stock market is going to do; one is reminded of the old and oft-quoted remark of J. P. Morgan, who was asked by an admirer what the future course of the stock market would be. He replied flatly: "It will fluctuate."

To analyze the market, one should begin with the line from *The Sound of Music*: "Let's start at the very beginning—a very good place to start." The beginning has to be the economy of the country.

Of course, the future of the economy may be no easier to diagnose than the future of the market. But anyone who invests without some thoughts about where the nation's economy will be six months to a year from then is investing in ignorance. This is not a book about how to invest; but one

* I am at present a member of the Board of Trustees of the University of Pennsylvania. I was not a trustee at the time of the reorganization. Outside of the fact that I once spent many hours commuting on its lines, I have never had any connection with the Penn Central.

should never invest in ignorance. Only after one has made up his mind about the economy—the core from which all else financial flows—should he make an investment in stocks. And, at that same time, a scrutiny of the bond market is highly advisable also. Rates of interest have an enormous impact on the price of stocks. Generally, as interest rates go up the stock market goes down, and vice versa. Obviously, this is not a correlation that one can count on from day to day, but the pattern is usually followed.

While the general outline of the economy in those critical times of May has already been described, a closer look is now necessary. At the time the nation had been trying to accomplish something that had never been achieved by any country in any period in history—in the old phrase, to have both guns and butter. As we know today, to our increased wisdom and sorrow, that probably is beyond the capacity of even the United States.

From 1965 to 1968 our expenditures for the Vietnam war had been rising at an extraordinary rate. Consciousness of the importance of such expenditures grew more slowly than the expenditures themselves. By the time everyone in the country understood the meaning of "cost effectiveness" and grasped the then almost incredible notion that there were some things, after all, that the country could not afford, it was too late to save us from the grisly experiences of 1969 and 1970.

No one knows exactly what Vietnam was costing or is costing annually. Such a computation is simply too mind-boggling to engage in or complete: if you use an aircraft 18% of the time in Vietnam, how much of its construction costs do you charge to the Vietnam war? Its operational cost? What about replacement costs—new designs, perhaps? Who keeps track of it all? Still, even admitting plenty of fuzziness around the edges of the issue, the generally accepted figure for 1968 and 1969 ran from $26.8- to $29.2-billion per year. At the time, the air was full of talk about a "peace dividend," meaning rather vaguely that as the Vietnam war wound down, the money being spent for it, practically dollar for dollar, would become available for those urgent domestic programs that everyone was becoming aware of. Ironically, though, the number and size of these programs seem to have risen so fast that the peace dividend has disappeared; at least nobody talks about it any more.

Vietnam was taking American lives and jeopardizing the national economy, as well as poisoning the national mood; a pledge to end it was clearly called for. Although he did not relate Vietnam to the economy, President Nixon gave that pledge in the 1968 campaign, in his inaugural speech, and repeatedly in the early years of his Administration. He pressed the pursuit of peace in Paris and pushed for "Vietnamization." At this writing, while the final outcome in Southeast Asia is highly uncertain, our withdrawal is assured. Also, the attitude of the country toward the war has changed as we have reduced the number of committed troops: the more highly pitched and emotional outcries against the war have subsided apace. No one likes the war, but few people decry it as loudly as before.

The drive toward social programs, however, remains strong. In the first year of the Nixon Administration, unrest and violence pocked the map of the United States. Programs for education, for slum clearance, for the relief of poverty, and many others aimed at improving "the quality of life," suddenly a popular phrase, tremendously accelerated in the face of that unrest. At the same time, a new consciousness dawned about the destruction of the environment, whose preservation was obviously a key ingredient in the concept of an improved "quality of life." Suddenly, the country was shocked by the deterioration of the environment and was more and more coming to understand the high cost of cleaning up streams, air and countryside.

One must agree with the sage who said that "a foolish consistency is the hobgoblin of little minds." For the taxpayer who was crying for social improvements and environmental protection was at the same time crying for tax relief. As is usually the case, the discussion of the new tax law in 1969 began with the sound premise that the existing jerry-built structure was full of holes and inequities and needed to be brought up to date. But what resulted was only another bit of patchwork. In terms of the fight against inflation, the Tax Reform Act of 1969 was a retrograde step, since income taxes were actually reduced. An increase would have taken money out of the economy and put it into the hands of the Federal Government; this would have had an anti-inflationary effect—as long as the Government did not turn around and spend all the money. But the net result of the tax reforms of 1969 was to allow inflation to run on unchecked. The tax surcharge clamped on a year earlier expired, too soon to have had any effect on inflation.

So other means for slowing the rate of inflation, which was still rising, had to be found. That put the emphasis on the money supply. In the various recessions of the last 25 years increases in the money supply had been the key element in speeding up the economy and putting it back on the road to recovery. The following chart demonstrates the point:

Changes in GNP in Relation to Money Supply

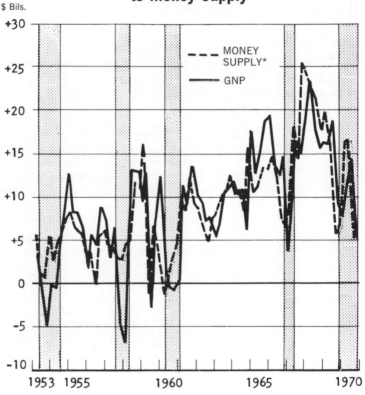

SOURCE: Monthly Economic Letter, First National City Bank, Feb. 1971.

*The money supply figures are adjusted to take into account changes in money supply during the preceding two years, with particular importance given to the preceding 6–9 month period.

Note: This chart confirms that changes in GNP in the main follow money supply changes by about 6–9 months. For the first six months of 1971 the money supply was $220 billion, while the GNP was $1,032 billion.

Now, money has many special properties of its own, but it also shares some properties with all other commodities. Money is no exception when it comes to the laws of supply and demand. The more of it there is, the less valuable it becomes, which is simply another way of saying that when you print money you create inflation. Although inflation had been a nettlesome problem since 1967, its intensity and stubbornness did not become obvious until 1969. We were in fact experiencing one of the worst inflations in recent history, certainly the worst since the Korean War. This inflation, more than any other, was due to the rising cost of services, which was in turn a rising proportion of the GNP itself. During the Korean War wage and price controls were imposed to check spiraling inflation. They were effective for a while, but after the war, prices began to soar. The experience of that time is cited by both proponents and opponents of price and wage controls to buttress their cases. The effects of the wage-price freeze of August 15, 1971, and the results of Phase Two, which has followed the 90-day freeze, are unlikely to settle this argument. Certainly Phase Two makes clear the great complexity of the economy, and the greater difficulties of governmental invasion of the private sector—however necessary.

Clearly a slowdown had to be forcibly induced in 1969. The Fed moved in to do just that. For 10 months there was no increase in the money stock. This tight-money policy was supported, at least in part, by some efforts—some say neither sufficiently prolonged nor very successful—toward fiscal conservatism. With those two brakes applied, the economy began slowly to grind to a halt.

During the 1960s the GNP had grown at a dramatic rate, moving from $503.7-billion at the end of 1960 to $931.4-billion at the end of 1969. But in the fourth quarter of 1969 the slowdown began. The GNP increased at an annual rate of only 3.3% compared to 7% and 8% in each of the four preceding quarters. The figure for the year ending with that period was only $942.8-billion, compared with $924.8-billion for the year ending in the second quarter. The rates of gain in the next two quarters were only 3.4% and 5.3%, the figures being $959.5-billion and $971.1-billion, respectively.

With that kind of drag, consumers, who make up the most difficult element to reach through governmental policies, at last began to feel the pinch. Consumer income, after years of dramatic rise, slowed to relatively small gains. Just look at the following table.

		Personal Income (In billions of dollars)
1960		401.0
1961		416.8
1962		442.6
1963		465.5
1964		497.5
1965		538.9
1966		587.2
1967		629.4
1968		688.9
1969	First Quarter	726.8
	Second Quarter	743.1
	Third Quarter	759.3
	Fourth Quarter	772.2
	For the Year	750.3
1970	First Quarter	784.3
	Second Quarter	803.8
	Third Quarter	809.8
	Fourth Quarter	816.7
	For the Year	803.6

Under such circumstances, the pocketbook nerve was clearly being touched. Reckless consumers can suddenly be transformed into cautious souls. At the time they reacted with their characteristic inbred conservatism. They became increasingly cautious buyers of just about everything. Worried about the future, which had looked such a lovely blushing pink only a year or so before, they began to reduce their borrowings and their installment credit purchases. Major appliances were especially hard hit.

The rate at which individuals save money, which is a critically important indicator, rose sharply. Curiously, even when they received pay increases, as government workers and many others did at this time, they did not step up their outlays. They simply saved more.

Wage increases now took on a new importance. Heretofore, it was generally accepted that union wages were not the true engine of inflation. Only a small percentage of total labor in the United States is unionized, the argument ran, and wage increases won by unions were, after all, only catching up with last year's inflation rate. Besides, the key figure is not wage

Personal Savings Rate Since 1960

Savings As a Percent of After-Tax Income

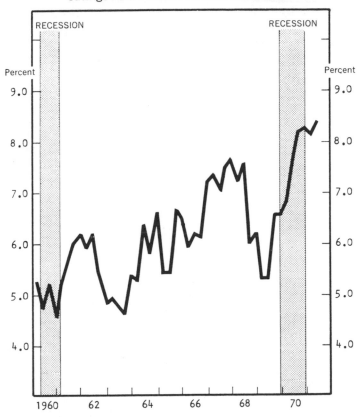

SOURCE: Morgan Guaranty Survey, August 1971.

rates but productivity rates, and productivity (**G**) in the United States in past years had been rising at a healthy rate—meaning faster than wages.

But now all this tilted. Wage increases, often forcibly won by strikes, raced ahead, and the inflation ceased being "demand pull" (**G**) and became "cost push" (**G**).

Of course, such wage increases, far in excess of increases in productivity and widening ever further from them, were alarming to everybody in the country who was not getting the

		Wages and Salaries (In billions of dollars)	Industrial Production Index (1957–59 equals 100)
1968	First Quarter	448.2	162.1
	Second Quarter	458.9	164.2
	Third Quarter	471.0	165.2
	Fourth Quarter	481.4	167.4
	For the Year	464.8	165.4
1969	First Quarter	491.6	170.2
	Second Quarter	502.9	172.8
	Third Quarter	516.4	174.3
	Fourth Quarter	525.3	172.8
	For the Year	509.0	172.8
1970	First Quarter	534.4	170.7
	Second Quarter	537.4	169.3
	Third Quarter	543.4	167.9
	Fourth Quarter	545.2	162.7
	For the Year	540.1	167.6
1971	First Quarter	560.2	165.2

increases—and that meant a majority of the people (see chart page 51). Pressure began to build for presidential action to prevent further wage increases, especially in the construction industry, where advances had been particularly outrageous.

The action that was often suggested was the imposition of wage and price controls—a very grave step, whose consequences would be very uncertain. The President's top economic advisers—Paul McCracken, George Shultz and others, recognized that wage increases were now a central cause of inflation, but nonetheless took a strong public stand against clamping on controls. They argued that such controls never had worked and could not work if tried at this juncture. Citing the precedent of the Korean War, they noted that all controls had done was to put a lid over boiling water; under the lid pressures continue to build, and eventually the steam was sure to blow. They also argued that since the Vietnam War was generally so unpopular, most Americans would not cooperate with the controls out of a sense of good citizenship, as they had during prior wars. Even during the Korean War, when there was broader agreement on the goals of the government, evasion and wage drift set in. Quality deterioration afflicted those products whose prices were subject to controls.

Not until more than a year later did the government's policy opposing controls change. The classic means for checking infla-

Wages, Productivity and Prices

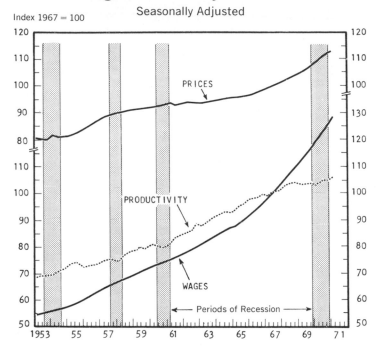

Index 1967 = 100   Seasonally Adjusted

SOURCE: The Conference Board Statistical Bulletin.

tion proved too slow; the Administration, much professional opinion outside of it (especially the Chairman of the Federal Reserve Board, Arthur Burns) and public sentiment all grew impatient. Thus to meet a new situation new restraints were imposed, including a wage-price freeze, a suspension of United States redemption of dollars in gold and an import surcharge on all dutiable products, on August 15, 1971. No one will ever know whether the classic methods, which economists generally believe must work if given time, would in the end have produced the desired results. My own judgment agrees with that of the Administration: I repeat, we live in a politico-economic world, which dictates pragmatic judgments, and the time for forceful action in August 1971 had come. But the means formerly being used to check inflation, had they by themselves been sustainable, might also have worked—and an important chunk would have been added to our economic knowledge. There is a great deal now about the free market that we'll never know. What we'll learn about peacetime economic controls may therefore be less useful.

Still, as investors came to consider whether or not to buy stocks back in late May 1970, they had to face the unhappy fact that the recession (G) and the slowdown in their own disposable personal income had not reduced the inflation rate in any way meaningful to the individual. The important signs at the time were read to indicate that the failing economy was going to continue, but that the purposes for which the downturn had been induced were not being achieved. The correctness of that view cannot be proved, and now that we have moved from freeze to Phase Two it never will be.

While President Nixon and his advisers resisted at the time the outcry for wage and price controls, they were equally determined to cure the inflationary sickness without killing the economic patient. The whole objective of the government's policy, of course, was to dampen the economy, not to drown it. The economy had to be slowed just to the point that inflation could be checked; then, we could take off the brakes.

This was kind of an experiment in brinkmanship. Few governments had ever managed this act successfully. No one had ever done it with an economy of the size and vitality of ours. The United States was on the roller coaster all right, and on the way down all right, but when we would get the last thrill, whip through the last dip and start up again, was beyond telling. Yet lots of investors in May 1970 must have agreed with the general thrust of the Nixon policy and must have believed in the "game plan," because they were buying, as we have seen—and they were buying the kinds of stocks that people usually tend to hold for long periods of time.

When a government seeks to let the air out of an overheated economy, it has to demonstrate its good faith and credibility. The single most convincing way to do that is by controlling its own expenditures. A big deficit in the Federal budget requires that large amounts of money be poured out into the economy, with an inflationary consequence. At the time, the Administration was quite properly emphasizing its intention to be fiscally responsible, or, in more precise terms, either to balance the budget or come close to balancing it. That note was sounded again in the declarations of August 1971.

As it turned out, though, there could have been no harder test of good intentions. Indeed, the events of 1970 raised the question whether an Administration can in the course of a couple of years get control over the government's expenditures. Many of the costs of government lie beyond any federal action: enormous costs are built into such programs as veterans' benefits, Medicare and Medicaid, farm price supports, interest on the national debt, and a host of other uncontrollables.

Where he could, President Nixon reached out to check expenditures. He reduced the Defense Department's budget by almost 10%, despite rising wages and prices, from 1968 to 1970. Prime contracts that were let by the Pentagon declined from an annual rate of $42.3-billion in 1968 to $34.1-billion in the first quarter of 1970 and to a rate of $28.4-billion during April and May. Plans were instituted to reduce the number of men in the armed forces by one million or more. In other areas the President vetoed a hospital construction bill, which he regarded as inflationary (only to have his veto overridden by the Congress). He also vetoed a major appropriation for the Department of Health, Education and Welfare because he felt the expenditures on education were too high. Later in the year he vetoed another education bill (again he was overridden) and a housing bill.

Thus, there emerged another kind of uncontrollable in the struggle against inflation—the will of the Congress. In mid-1970, the President took to television and radio in an attempt to marshal public opinion against the acts of the Congress, some of which he regarded as irresponsible. But the steam behind social programs was simply too great. While the economy slowed in the third quarter of 1970 and the GNP had an actual absolute net decline in the fourth quarter, the budget did not come close to being balanced. Now we know that the budgetary deficit for fiscal 1970–71 reached $23.2-billion. About the same amount, or more, is forecast for fiscal 1971–72.

But the investor in the stock market, especially the one who was buying those long-range growth stocks, certainly should have been, and probably was, looking beyond the next couple of quarters. In May 1970 he ought to have had his eye on the economic prospects for 1971, which promised to be far more favorable than the current period. Intervening, of course, would be the mid-term elections of 1970, when the entire House of Representatives, one-third of the Senate and a flock of key governorships all came up for election. If the elections should turn out favorably for the Administration, that would have many economic implications, and so implications for the investor; on the other hand, a smashing defeat for the President's party might perhaps lead to quite different conclusions in terms of investment. And the Cambodian question continued to hang over the whole outlook. As it turned out, the Republican losses of state houses proved most damaging to the GOP; but the Cambodian incursion, even while it was ending, probably had an even greater effect.

To demonstrate the connection between Cambodia and the stock markets, which we noted earlier, and to show the dangers inherent in predicting the general course of the market, let me retrace my steps to recount an anecdote that goes back to that White House meeting on April 29. You will recall that among those invited from the financial world were some Wall Street leaders. Also present were the President's chief economic advisers, Paul McCracken and Herbert Stein, and White House assistants John Ehrlichman and Peter Flanigan. During one of those forward-looking discussions that everybody who cares about markets loves to have, a member of the White House staff asked me for my market forecast— "theoretical," of course. I indicated that one of the great imponderables in any such forecast was the future of Vietnam. But I went on to say, prompted by one of the other brokers present, that any move into neighboring areas such as Cambodia would probably touch off a sell-off and drive the market down. None of the President's advisers, some of whom I assume knew what was about to happen, commented.

Later that morning, at 11:25 A.M. on April 29, the news of the invasion was made public. Immediately after the announcement hit the Dow Jones broad tape (G), the market sold off for a brief period. After that downward wiggle, however, nothing much more happened. Somewhat later, the market began to rally and by the end of the day it was up a total of 13.06 points on a volume of 15.8-million shares.

After the close of business one of the President's aides called me and said, "Didn't you say that the market would move strongly as a result of the Cambodian news—probably down?" Rather ruefully, I had to admit that I had said so. I think the White House aide took a little pleasure in telling me—I was at the time the president and chief operating officer of Merrill Lynch and had spent 24 years in the brokerage business— that the President of the United States was a better market forecaster than I. He reminded me that the President had told the group of businessmen in the White House on April 28 that "if I had any money I would be buying." Now the market was up, and the President's hypothetical investments looked pretty good. All I could say was, "Wait and see."

Well, as of this writing, the President's hypothetical investments still look good. He had quite correctly identified a good time to buy. But, as it turned out, I was right, too. The market sell-off began the next day as the implications of the Cambodian situation, and more particularly the highly emotional national reaction to it, began to dawn. As we've noted, the eastern press in the United States led the way, but elsewhere in the country, as well as abroad, a hue and cry of an unexpected intensity was raised. Despite the President's pledge that this was only a brief incursion for a specific military purpose, the belief spread that we were in Cambodia for an indefinite length of time. The market plunged. In two weeks the Dow Jones industrials fell to 693.84, some 43.55 points below the close on the invasion date. Then it paused until the three days in May.

That experience of the month just past was still deeply affecting investors during the week of May 25. And brokers, whose market views can often change the course of the market, were brooding over such matters as the slowdown in housing starts, the consumer's persistent tendency to hold onto his money, and the general economic climate already described. The consumer's caution had become very pronounced during the pre-Easter season, which had been a poor one for retail sales.

Truisms are a bore, but they are not without their point. The relevant truism at this instance is that you can never know for sure that "this is the time to buy." The keenest minds on Wall Street cannot identify the perfect moment to plunge. Only in retrospect can you recognize such times without a quiver of doubt. Then, it is easy enough to point to the chart and say, "Here is where I should have been buying" or "That was the point to sell."

With hindsight, the lessons of history are lucid.

CHAPTER IV

Money's Influence

LOOKING BACK FROM TODAY'S PROMONTORY, some years that seemed pretty gray for investing, and indeed pretty gray for the whole American future, now look positively golden. Tables that show wisdom are impossible to draw. But the two left-hand columns that follow show the Dow Jones Averages in years when pessimism was deep-rooted; the columns on the right, when optimism was sprouting. In both sets of years—both the pessimistic and the optimistic—excellent reasons abounded for the then-current mood. But still better reasons changed the mood—and the prices.

The Mood and the Averages

Pessimistic Year	DJ Industrial Low	Optimistic Year	DJ Industrial High
1934	85.51	1937	194.40
1942	92.92	1946	212.50
1949	161.60	1952	292.00
1954	279.87	1956	521.05
1957	419.79	1960	685.47

After the sell-off following the assassination of President Kennedy, the market embarked on its longest and steadiest climb in history. The rise continued until December 1968, except for a brief pause in 1966. Then the trend reversed, and prices slid, hitting bottom and—as we know from our present vantage point—starting up again in May 1970.

Yet individual stocks and individual investment situations may move without much reference to the course that other securities are taking. When you look at the stock exchange tables in a newspaper, no matter what kind of day it has been, you will always find some stocks with that pleasant-looking plus sign in the net change column. Still, trends are important and do persist. One of the most reliable ways of anticipating the trend of stock prices, as I've said, is by forecasting the coming movements in the economy; historically, the correlation is quite clear.

But, as with everything else about the market, there is a catch—not quite so baffling as Catch-22, but a catch nonetheless. The catch is that the economy's future isn't easy to read. And in this context the catch is harder still to get by, because one must also determine just what kind of indicator the market is. Does it reflect the economy as the economy will be three months from the present? Six months from the present? Or a year from the present? The puzzle is something of a double one—analyzing where the economy is going, and then analyzing what the lag is between the economy and the market. The widely accepted estimate now says that the market tells us what is going to happen in the economy over the next six months. That estimate may be generally true. But "generally," of course, is the operative word.

If we accept the six-month theory, then we can conclude that the intelligent investor in May 1970 was looking, or should have been looking, at the economy of November 1970. If he was doing that, he had good reason to expect an upturn. In May, virtually every economist was predicting that by the end of the year every facet of the economy would be brighter.

As it turned out, the economy had receded by the end of the year, but the year-end was full of good omens—and, again looking ahead from *then*, the market should have been moving up. As I have noted earlier, the big thrust of buying came from individuals, and it seems safe to conclude that the individuals at the time were peering into the future and liked what they saw. Present fears were canceled out by future hopes.

For many reasons, one of which is that superficially at least it is easier to understand, the stock market has always influenced the public more than the bond market (**G**) has. One of the most important developments of 1970 was the upsurge of interest in the bond market by individuals. It would be going too far to say that the individual cared nothing about the bond market formerly, but the fact is that 1970 did mark a watershed in the bond market's history. A man with $5,000 or $10,000 to invest in 1970, at least for part of the year, took a close look at the bond market as well as at the stock market —and that new awareness of investment possibilities constituted, in my opinion, a new awakening.

For the bond market and the stock market to move together is an unusual occurrence. But early in that month of May that is exactly what was happening. Stock prices were deteriorating. Oddly enough, bond prices were doing precisely the same thing. But for new investors, of course, that meant that rates of return on bonds were becoming more attractive.

Falling Prices Equal Rising Yields

Yield	Price
6 %	$1,000.00
6 1/8	985.70
6 1/4	971.70
6 3/8	957.90
6 1/2	944.50
6 5/8	931.30
6 3/4	918.30
6 7/8	905.70
7	893.20

Yields on bonds started up, which is to say the prices started down, in the fall of 1968. So the bond market hit a low point at that time while the stock market was at a high—a common coincidence. Three months later, the stock market began its downward trend—another way of saying that the bond market anticipated the stock market by three months. All during 1969, while stocks were slipping more and more, bond prices also continued to decline—and yields on bonds continued to rise. A slight dip occurred early in the spring of 1970, but by May, interest rates were close to their all-time high.

That was true not only of interest paid on bonds but of rates on commercial loans, consumer loans, mortgages and other types of borrowings. Not since the Civil War have such high levels of interest prevailed: one Aaa utility, New Jersey Bell Telephone, offered bonds at 9.35%, an unheard-of yield. Such returns stirred doubts about the stock market—doubts particularly easy to stir at a time when prices were coming down and when disillusionment was spreading. Savings banks paying 5% or better capitalized on the current psychology by publicizing the returns compounded on a deposit left with them and by driving home their point with advertisements asking the consumer, in effect, "Why gamble?"

To ascertain why interest rates had reached such lofty peaks, we must track back to Government fiscal and monetary policy. In the recent past, the fiscal school—that group which believed that the primary force in the economy was action by the Federal Government in taking money away from its citizens in the form of taxation and putting it back into the economy in the form of expenditures—had clearly been in the ascendancy. As disciples of Lord Keynes, they assumed positions of key importance in the New Deal, the New Frontier, and finally in the Great Society. Democratic administrations had come to accept as unquestioned truth the proposition that proper manipulation of the Federal budget could spell prosperity.

At one time it had been considered a sign of national disgrace to have a budgetary deficit. The old household analogy was often cited: you can't spend more than you make, or you'll end up in jail. But the arguments of New Deal economists were gradually gaining acceptance. The arguments showed that the parallels between the Government and the family are far from accurate: families have to make their money, while governments can print theirs. In a depression, prime the pump by printing money and spending it; after all, the country is going to be around for quite a while, and the Government might as well spend now, run up deficits and help people in distress. Better to accomplish worthwhile social programs now, rather than to have the country becalmed in a slack tide, waiting for a few business leaders to get back their courage and borrow money to build new plants and buy new equipment—at least so ran the argument.

A political foundation of course supported this economic edifice. In the post-World War II era, when the economy was slow, politicians quite naturally fell happily on any credible theory that also made it possible for them to spend Government funds. The old slogan popularly attributed to Harry Hopkins, "We shall spend and spend, tax and tax, elect and elect," had a great political appeal. It also made some good economic sense.

In very recent years, as opposed to past history, however, that very fine and very convenient philosophy of the fiscalists found a formidable challenger. The new school of economic

philosophers, who call themselves "monetarists," is led by
Milton Friedman of the University of Chicago. Along with
Anna Schwartz, Friedman wrote a monumental study entitled *A Monetary History of the United States,* which was to
become a Bible for all Friedmanites. The study traced the
movements of the money stock, as enlarged or contracted by
the Federal Reserve Board, and correlated those movements
with the state of the economy. Its conclusion was that it was
really only the money supply and its expansion or contraction
that spelled prosperity and depression, inflation and deflation
(see chart page 46 giving changes in the money supply).

Further, the monetarists, whose leading institution outside
of the University of Chicago is the Federal Reserve Bank of
St. Louis, began to trace virtually every economic and financial development back to the money supply. Through the person of the brilliant and pugnacious Dr. Friedman, they argued
that the effect of fiscal policies on the course of the economy
and the individual American had been greatly exaggerated.
Monographs in support of this argument have poured in tor-
rents from the Federal Reserve Bank of St. Louis, and from
other monetarist strongholds. Some of them related stock market movements to money supply in a very persuasive correlation, principally worked out by Dr. Beryl W. Sprinkel, now
senior vice president and chief economist of the Harris Trust &
Savings Bank in Chicago.

Also important among monetarist studies is Michael Keran's
study in the *Review of the Federal Reserve Bank of St. Louis,*
published in November 1969. This study, which updated an
earlier one in the same publication in November 1968 by
Leonall Andersen and Jerry Jordan, entitled *Monetary and
Fiscal Actions—A Test of Their Relative Importance on
Economic Stabilization,* reviewed the relative importance of
monetary and fiscal policies for the economy for 50 years,
from 1919 to 1969. The study demonstrated, to the entire
satisfaction of its authors anyway and to the satisfaction of
many others as well, that of the two influences on the economy—fiscal and monetary—the monetary is by far the more
important.

For example, during the period from 1919 to 1929, a
period of general economic prosperity, the study shows that
there were three cyclical declines. Each of those declines,
which came in 1920–21, 1923–24, and 1927, was matched
by a corresponding movement in the money stock of a restrictive nature. But, in contrast to such cycles, Federal Gov-

ernment spending showed very little fluctuation in the same decade. Conclusion: the money stock is the heart of the matter as far as the body economic goes.

Nor is the correlation limited to that one decade. Keran shows the same conclusions can be drawn for subsequent declines in economic activity, for example the declines in 1929, in 1933 and in 1937–38. He also demonstrates that the recovery in the intervening years can be explained in the same way, by the functioning of the same mechanism. The money supply actually declined from late 1929 through 1931, but it increased at the end of 1933, the first increase since the third quarter of 1929. Economic activity exactly paralleled the pattern of growth in the money stock. But, according to Keran, fiscal influences over the same period were quite erratic. Sometimes they were expansionary, sometimes restrictive, sometimes they conformed to monetary influences and sometimes they counterbalanced them. But the economy was evidently unmoved by such fiscal change: in every case, it moved consistently with the direction and magnitude of monetary influences. More recent experience reinforces the point, although the debate is not ended yet.

The only time when the money stock did not move in absolute correlation with the economy was in 1951. That was the only deceleration in economic activity, in the entire 50-year period studied, which came about while the money stock was expanding. Once in 50 years would seem a permissible aberration. But, once aroused, Friedman and Schwartz were prepared to explain even that one exception. They point out that in March of 1951, the Treasury Department and the Federal Reserve agreed that the Fed could abandon its wartime policy of pegging the price of Government bonds to keep them on an even keel. (Although the Fed did not move immediately in this respect, it finally did abandon its active support of the Government bond market.) That abandonment reduced the apparent liquidity and caused the aberration, the only one in the statistical series.

All this is pregnant with meaning for investors. If you can perceive that changes in the money stock (in this case defined as all public holdings of coin and currency outside of banks plus demand deposits [G]) clearly foreshadow changes in economic activity, then you should be wiser about your investments. But obviously you must know when a change in the money stock has taken place or is taking place.

Such changes are made by the Federal Reserve Board

through its Open Market Committee (**G**). But this too has its subtleties. The Fed does not have the tools to control movements in money and bank credit with any high degree of precision in the short run. Many factors beyond the Fed's control may offset what the Fed is trying to do over a brief period of time. Precise statistics on what is going on out there in the market do not come in instantaneously, and are not always easy to interpret. Day to day and week to week open market operations cannot be finely tuned to offset opposing outside influences that may exist.

So, for practical reasons, when you study the money supply you are already studying history. And you cannot draw conclusions from studying the data from week to week. A better span would cover perhaps three months, which gives you a much better indicator as a moving average (**G**). With a three-month overview, you are able to get a much better idea of what it is that the money managers are trying to accomplish.

Obviously, the longer the course the better. If you can determine a six-month indicator or a year's indicator, you will have hit on something pretty good. But what that will tell you about the future is harder to decide. Obviously, you cannot assume that the policy for the last six months will be the policy for the next six. You can read statements of Government policy by members of the Fed and by politicians for some insight, and you may hit it right. But there is no guarantee.

A dig into the Fed's activities for 1969 turns up some interesting food for thought. The Open Market Committee is composed of seven members of the Board of Governors of the Federal Reserve System and five of the 12 district Federal Reserve Bank presidents. The other seven presidents attend meetings of the Open Market Committee, and participate in the deliberations, but they do not have a vote. Except for the president of the New York Federal Reserve Bank, who because of the importance of his district is a permanent member of the Open Market Committee, membership rotates among the presidents of the other districts, changing each March. The Chairman of the Fed, by the way, is a member of the Open Market Committee—but in that committee, as elsewhere, he has only one vote.

During 1969 the Fed's Open Market Committee met 14 times—once a month, with two meetings in April and two meetings in October.* The minutes of the meetings, which are now available, indicate that besides determining the policy of increasing or decreasing the money stock, the committee discussed changes in spending, industrial production indices, price studies, international developments, extent of current Treasury financing, the Federal budget and a report on interest rates, as well as other measures of money market conditions and monetary aggregates. That adds up to a lot of important topics.

All of this information ultimately appears in the *Federal Reserve Bulletin,* a public document. But the *Bulletin* does not come out early enough to be of much help to speculators. Each spring the Board of Governors of the Federal Reserve System also issues an Annual Report giving an account of all of their significant meetings. The Federal Reserve Bank in New York is in charge of actual market operations through recognized Government bond dealers, because New York is the financial headquarters of the country and therefore the place where Government bond dealings are conducted.

On page 64 appears a list of the Government bond dealers reporting to the Market Statistics Division of the Federal Reserve Bank of New York.

In principle, the Federal Reserve Board is independent of the current administration in Washington. Interestingly, neither in journalism nor elsewhere, at least in the recent past, has this principle to my knowledge been subject to serious challenge or public debate. Generally, there is widespread acceptance of the concept that independence is wise and sound. Attention is largely centered around the degree of the independence, rather than around the merits of it. Usually, one hears that the Fed is "under pressure" from the Administration or the Congress. The implication is that the Fed should "resist" this pressure.

In fact, a case can be made that the Fed should be subordinate to the Administration, so that two separate economic policies would not be working at cross-purposes. Such cross-purposes were running late in the Johnson Administration when, after a long struggle, a surcharge was belatedly tacked

---

* Present were Messrs. Alfred Hayes (New York), Monroe Kimbrel (Atlanta), Frank E. Morris (Boston), W. Braddock Hickman (Cleveland), and Hugh D. Galusha Jr. (Minneapolis). Beginning March 4, the rotating members were Messrs. Charles J. Scanlon (Chicago), Philip E. Coldwell (Dallas), George H. Clay (Kansas City), and Carl R. Bopp (Philadelphia).

Government Securities Dealers Reporting to the Federal Reserve Bank of New York

Bankers Trust Company
Briggs, Schaedle & Company, Inc.
The Chase Manhattan Bank, N.A.
Chemical Bank
Continental Illinois National Bank & Trust Company of Chicago
Discount Corporation of New York
F. I. du Pont, Glore Forgan & Company
The First Boston Corporation
First National Bank of Chicago
First National City Bank
Harris Trust and Savings Bank
Aubrey G. Lanston & Company, Inc.
Merrill Lynch, Pierce, Fenner & Smith Inc.
Morgan Guaranty Trust Company of New York
New York Hanseatic Corporation
William E. Pollock & Company, Inc.
Chas. E. Quincey & Company
Salomon Brothers
Second District Securities Company, Inc.
United California Bank

NOTE: This list has been compiled and made available for statistical purposes only and has no significance with respect to other relationships between dealers and the Federal Reserve Bank of New York. New organizations may have joined this group since this list was compiled.

onto the tax structure. Despite this effort to take money out of the economy, however, the Fed continued to pump money into it. (William McChesney Martin Jr., then Chairman of the Fed, later admitted that this was one of the most serious mistakes made by the Fed in the recent past.) As a consequence of the divergent policies of the Administration and the Fed, the advantages of the tax increase as a check on inflation—an advantage that the monetarists of course would judge to be at best only marginal—were canceled out by increases in the money stock. Presumably, had the Fed been less independent at that time, economic policies might have worked better. But one could also argue that President Nixon's sweeping economic decrees of August 1971 came about in part at least because Arthur Burns, Martin's successor at the Fed, argued so strongly for them—in a reassertion of the independence of his position.

In January 1969, however, the two autonomous bodies, that is the Fed on the one hand and the new Republican Administration on the other, were moving on parallel tracks. The Republican Administration made a policy decision that the battle against inflation took priority over every other economic consideration. And the Open Market Committee, under the direction of the Federal Reserve Board, was in full agreement. The minutes published later revealed that at the meeting of the Open Market Committee on January 14, the committee stated flatly that "in this situation it is the policy of the Federal Open Market Committee to foster financial conditions conducive to the reduction of inflationary pressures, with a view to encouraging a more substantial rate of economic growth and attaining reasonable equilibrium in the country's balance of payments." Mr. Morris of Boston was a lone dissenter—because he felt the directive, as adopted, "could be consistent with an unduly restrictive monetary policy." But with independent-minded people such as those on the Committee, a single dissenter meant virtual unanimity—in short, the start of activities to squeeze the money supply.

In its operating instructions the Open Market Committee stated "to implement this policy [of restriction], open market operations until the next meeting of the Committee shall be conducted with a view to maintaining the prevailing firm conditions in money and short term credit markets." There was one proviso—the so-called " . . . Proviso Clause of Directive" —which ran as follows: "provided however that operations shall be modified to the extent permitted by the forthcoming Treasury refunding, if bank credit expansion appears to be deviating significantly from current projections."

Meanwhile, in his public statements the President was repeatedly stressing that the time had come for fiscal responsibility and that his administration's contribution to the anti-inflationary effort was going to be a balanced budget. So harmony about the advisability of the anti-inflation policy was widespread, at least as far as members of the administration and the Fed were concerned. Thus encouraged, the Open Market Committee stuck to its guns: at meetings on February 4, March 4 and April 1 it held fast to the earlier policy statement, and screwed the lid on money down tight.

At the April 1 meeting, some cracks in the column appeared when two members of the Open Market Committee dissented: Messrs. Coldwell and Maisel.

Interestingly, the two dissented for different reasons. Coldwell wanted the Fed to take an even sterner tack. He favored tightening reserve requirements and increasing the discount rate so that there would be more visible symbols of the Fed's restrictive policy. Maisel, by contrast, favored a more gradualist approach. He was concerned that the Committee was paying too much attention to interest rates and not enough to the supply of money in measuring the results of its policies. He felt the effect of the Fed's policy, as then being carried out, would actually be to diminish the money supply rather than simply to keep it constant, as was the Committee's stated intent.

In meetings on April 29 and May 27, unanimity was restored. On June 24 only Mr. Maisel dissented from a continuation of this rigid refusal to put more dollars out to chase more goods. On July 15—still no change.

The first indication that this long dry spell, extending for a virtually unprecedented period from January onwards, might be ending came on August 12. At that time a subtle change was made in the consensus. The minutes setting out the policy began as follows: "With a view to encouraging sustainable economic growth . . ." The word "more," formerly included, was dropped from the former phrase "more sustainable economic growth." The intention was to avoid the implication that a reduced rate of growth in real Gross National Product might be sustainable over the long run. But the Open Market Committee, despite this delicate shift in course, still did not change its standing instructions to the Federal Reserve Bank of New York.

So the months clicked by with the Fed standing like a rock. For the balance of the year, no significant deviation was recorded. Mr. Maisel and Mr. Mitchell, another member, sporadically dissented, but the basic policy remained in force.

The Fed's determination made a remarkable year all the more remarkable. In the first six months of 1969 the money stock dropped from $201.7-billion in January to $197-billion at the end of June; in the second six months it finally got back to $201-billion in November and reached $206-billion at year-end. What might be called ZMG, for zero money growth, was a cold shower for an overheated economy.

Such stunting of the growth in the monetary aggregate carried with it, after a rather brief time lag, progressively tighter money markets. What are known as Federal funds (**G**) began to rise dramatically. Short-term money rates (three-month Treasury bills) rose from 6.21% on January 18, 1969, to

6.66% by the end of June. By July 26, in a surge that made headline news in all of the financial columns, three-month bills moved to 7.22%. By November 29, they reached 7.47%, and on December 20 they hit 7.92%. The high point was reached January 3, 1970, when they hit 8.09%. That is an enormously high rate of interest on securities guaranteed by the Federal Government. In late December 1971, the rate was below 4%.

Corporate bonds were moving upward in tandem with government paper. In December 1968 Aaa-rated corporate bonds were paying an interest rate of 6.18%. The direction was clearly upward: at mid-year Aaa corporates were paying 6.98%. By December 1969, just before the period we are talking about, they were up to 7.72%. Three-month Treasury bills on the same date were paying 5.33%. Moving commensurately were long-term rates: in June 1969, 6.43%; by December 1969, 7.81%.

In the first four months of 1970 the rates continued this rapid climb. Short-term rates, which flagged slightly during March and April, also headed back upwards in May. On June 15 the highest yield ever paid on an Aaa issue caused a buzz in the financial community. The issue, for which Merrill Lynch was the managing underwriter, was New Jersey Bell Telephone, which paid the nigh unbelievable amount of 9.35% for a $100-million issue due in the year 2010. At the same time, an A-rated issue of an electric utility was priced to yield 10%. An A-rated issue of a blue chip corporation, RCA, was put out at 9.25%, the highest rate ever recorded for an A-rated industrial corporate bond.

Besides the yields that those bonds were paying, the unprecedented participation of individuals in the bond market marked another milestone. The New Jersey Bell issue just mentioned, for example, sold out quickly—with a very high share of these bonds, in this case about 60% of the issue being bought by individuals. People were aware that such astronomical heights for yields presented a once-in-a-decade opportunity —or perhaps once-in-a-lifetime—and they were acting to take advantage of the moment. They were taking their money out of banks, savings and loan institutions, drawing down the equity in life insurance policies, and generally putting together their liquid assets to invest them directly in bonds. This table shows why bond yields in general at the time were very attractive, especially for people in the upper tax brackets:

Bond Yields

(PERCENT PER ANNUM)

		Tax-Exempt State and Local, Aaa	Corporate Aaa
1965		3.16	4.49
1966		3.67	5.13
1967		3.74	5.51
1968		4.20	6.18
1969		5.45	7.03
1970	January	6.38	7.91
	February	6.19	7.93
	March	5.81	7.84
	April	6.24	7.83
	May	6.70	8.11
	June	6.81	8.48
	July	6.40	8.44
	August	5.96	8.13
	September	5.90	8.09
	October	6.07	8.03
	November	5.79	8.05
	December	5.21	7.64
	Average for the Year	6.12	8.04

NOTE: Annual yields are averages of monthly or quarterly data.

In looking at that table, you should bear in mind the meaning to higher income people of those tax-exempt yields. The Minneapolis-St. Paul metropolitan area, for example, had an Aa-rated municipal bond issue at this time which sold at an interest cost of 6.94%. Bonds that were of longer maturity, namely the ones due to be paid off in 1990, were offered at 7.30%. For someone in the 50% income tax bracket, that was as good as a yield of nearly 15% in taxable income.

Interest rates had not hit such high levels since the Civil War. And when you consider that this rise was taking place at the same time that the stock market was dropping sharply, you can understand why investors in the market were shaking their heads—or their fists.

Banks and business corporations, too, were engaged in a struggle to adjust to these ever-tightening monetary conditions. American banks went abroad, principally into the Euro-dollar (G) market, in a widening search for cheaper money.

Growth in Commercial Paper and Eurodollar Markets

(Debt Outstanding)

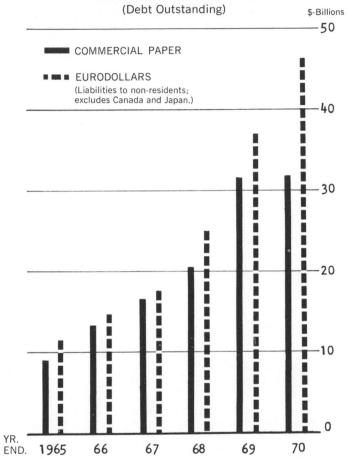

$-Billions

SOURCE: Federal Reserve Board & Bank of International Settlements.

The strategy worked for a while; then, the new demand forced up Eurodollar rates to American levels.

Another way for corporations to meet these extraordinarily difficult conditions, which were characterized as a "money crunch," was through the issuance of commercial paper (**G**). Where there had been only a small commercial paper market before, there sprung up a market estimated in May 1970, a high point, to be greater than $39-billion, compared with $4.5-billion in 1960 and $921-million in 1950.

The chart on page 69 depicts the sudden mushrooming of the Eurodollar market and the commercial paper market. It also illustrates the imagination of financial people, particularly corporate treasurers and investment bankers, who when under stress showed a remarkable ability to invent new financial instruments.

Finally, the point was reached where the "money crunch" was actually threatening to crunch everyone to dust. The traditional relationships between all of the financial institutions were being distorted. Disintermediation (**G**), encouraged by the downturn in the stock market, was having seriously damaging consequences. The marketplace no longer could be relied on to direct an orderly flow of funds, since the normal channels had been twisted beyond recognition by the extraordinary forces at work. Marine animals can live under enormous pressure, but not unlimited pressure; if you increase sufficiently the weight of the column of water above them, life is no longer possible. Something like that increase was threatening the financial mechanisms on which so much of our economy depends.

A clear case in point is what happened to the savings and loan institutions. These centers for the lending of mortgage money, on which in turn so many hopes and houses rest, were in many cases forbidden by law or regulation to match the high rates that the market offered. People who had money on deposit in savings and loan associations simply moved it to places where the interest rates were higher—with the result that very little mortgage money was available. Many savings and loan institutions, unable to meet the competition, were threatened with extinction. And the dearth of mortgage money obviously has important social and political implications, as well as economic significance.

Late in 1969 there were preliminary indications that the Open Market Committee of the Fed was contemplating a substantial change in policy. Corporate liquidity had been squeezed, and the banks were short of funds—but these were not the main causes behind the Fed's decision. The principal reason for a shift in course came from the fact that the calculated effect of the no-growth policy, a slowdown in the economy, had been achieved.

In September 1969 industrial production, a very important indicator measuring the economy's output of goods, declined for the second month in a row. In a clearly related trend, unemployment was on the rise. In the preceding month it had gone up from 3.5% to 3.8%—a 9% increase. In discussing general economic conditions on December 16, 1969, the staff of the Open Market Committee predicted that real growth in the Gross National Product would be halted by the fourth quarter—that is, the quarter then already in progress, for which, of course, even preliminary figures would not be available for another month or two. Looking further ahead, the staff predicted little or no rise in the real rate of growth of the Gross National Product in the first half of 1970. The members of the Open Market Committee were doubtless also aware of a growing wave of protest against their restrictive policies, which, although necessary, were also causing nationwide hardships.

Finally, the several elements that marked the time for a change fell into place. On January 15, 1970, the Open Market Committee altered its course. The minutes read: "The Committee concluded that in the conduct of open market operations, increased stress should be placed on the objectives of achieving modest growth in the monetary aggregate with about equal weight being given to bank credit and the money stock." Generally, the decision amounted to an agreement that while "firm conditions," meaning continued restrictions, should be maintained in the money markets, some increase in the money stock could be allowed. This view was supported by the premise widely accepted by Friedmanites and other economists that changes in the money supply affect the economy only after the passage of a considerable interval, probably more than six months. That meant, of course, that the inhibiting effect of tight money, already showing in some sectors of the economy, would presently have more and more force in these and other areas. Further, changes in the direction of liberalization would be felt months later, just about the time when the economy would need the stimulus.

So, following the watershed decisions taken by the Open Market Committee on January 15, the money supply started to grow at an annual rate of about 5%. It continued at that rate for the first six months of 1970. Then the rate of increase speeded up.

All changes in the increase of the money stock were and are closely monitored. But watching the dials is not the same as controlling the vehicle. To maintain an absolutely steady rate of monetary growth—metaphorically, to keep the needle at the precise rate of speed you want to go and to travel indefinitely at that speed—is impossible. Examples are readily at hand. In a letter to Senator William Proxmire in March 1970, the new Chairman of the Fed, Arthur Burns, indicated that a 4% growth rate was about what he wanted to achieve. But there was a large Treasury refunding program (**G**) already scheduled for April. Also, besides the refunding, there was the adverse effect on the money market of the Cambodian invasion. So, despite Dr. Burns' prediction to Senator Proxmire, the money supply actually grew at an annual rate of 10.2% for the three months from March 1 to the end of May 1970. That rate is not sustainable for very long without a great inflationary effect.

Looking back over recent years, then, you have to conclude that the Fed had been steering a mighty erratic course. In the late Johnson years there had been a rapid increase in the money supply. As soon as the Nixon Administration took the wheel, it let up on the throttle and then came down hard on the brakes. But at least in part because of external forces that could not be controlled, the accelerator then went down once more. "Fasten seat belts" was a good precautionary measure. That stop-and-go course, with its far-reaching effects, was very much on the minds of the investors in May 1970.

Thus do events distant from Wall Street create changes of 1/8 and 1/4 point—or more.

The experiences of 1970 also provided some interesting tests for the monetarists' school of thought. One of the first lessons learned in this great experiment—and it was an experiment such as no other industrial country had ever launched—was that nothing very effective or very fundamental can be accomplished very quickly with the monetary instruments. The strength and the momentum of inflation and inflationary expectations had clearly been underestimated. When people have fresh evidence that makes frugality seem purposeless, they are going to spend more—regardless of exhortation. The belief that the same can of peas would cost more next year than this year was ingrained by that time. And no quick turn in the economy could root out that belief in a short time.

Furthermore, even all of the power of the Fed was not enough to turn down interest rates quickly. The time lags between policy changes and the results of policy changes were long. Inflation had its claws in the economy far deeper than anyone had realized.

Vital at this point were public understanding and governmental credibility. To knock down inflationary expectations, the administration more than anything else had *to be believed.* So, in speech after speech, the key spokesmen for the administration—the then Secretary of the Treasury David Kennedy, the Chairman of the Council of Economic Advisers Paul McCracken, Arthur Burns of the Federal Reserve and even Attorney General John Mitchell—set out to explain what the administration was doing and why it was bound to work. The group became known to insiders as "Gideon's Army."

But the army's effort could not rapidly check the basic forces already in motion. Interest rates are not amenable to oral persuasion. So, on June 17, 1970—five months after the Fed changed its course—President Nixon himself took a hand. In an address to the nation, the President stressed the fact that the Government had embarked on expansionary policies, and had ended the period of tight money. The President acknowledged that inflation was still a serious problem, but he predicted that the rate of inflation would decline as the restrictive policies recently applied began to take effect. "It's a little like trying to bring a boat into a dock," he said. "You turn down the power well before you get to the dock, and let the boat coast in." The President was obviously trying to restore confidence in the American economy in the wake of the stock market decline of the previous month. But he was also hoping to bring about a break in the high interest rates that discourage economic expansion. He noted that the money supply had increased by 6% over the past six months, and he assured his audience that the Fed intended to supply enough money so that "the orderly expansion of the economy will not be endangered."

As it turned out, interest rates did begin to decline soon after the President's address. On July 22 the Bell Telephone Company of Pennsylvania, an Aaa-rated utility, floated a $100-million issue, priced at 8.50%, 85 basis points (G) below the yield on the Aaa-rated New Jersey Bell issue, which had been sold just five weeks earlier. In July New York State sold a $60-million issue, which was the same quality of an almost identical issue put out by the State of Wisconsin in May. But now the New York State issue drew a yield 1.01% lower than that of Wisconsin—a comment on the market, rather than on the relative financial conditions of the two states.

The yield on Federal funds was also dropping rapidly. At the end of December 1969 the interest rate for Federal funds was 8.97%. On May 2, 1970, the rate was 8.43%, and by September 26, 1970, Federal funds were down to 5.84%. This very strong indicator showed how quickly interest rate trends, which had been so long abuilding, can reverse themselves.

CHAPTER V

Inside the Market

AGAINST THAT BACKGROUND, MOVEMENTS IN the stock market plotted over the same couple of years can be better understood. Back on December 3, 1968, the Dow Jones Industrial Average hit a high of 990.99. At the beginning of 1969, the first session of the new year saw the Dow Jones go up by almost four points—the strongest gain since the previous December 3. About that time, a few farsighted men saw that the Federal Reserve was about to crack down and impose the deflationary measures that were so long overdue. Tilford Gaines, a vice president and economist for the Manufacturers Hanover Trust, predicted that the Fed intended to "create a credit crunch" on commercial banks. He told businessmen that they were badly miscalculating consumer demand for their products as they rushed to build inventories. They were, he said, overstocking inventories and increasing their productive capacities much too fast. He warned that business behavior and consumer behavior were on a collision course.

Many other realistic economists echoed the same general theme. Inflation was outrunning prosperity; corporate profits were bound to suffer. ("With common stocks, it's earnings. That's the name of the game," said economist Paul Samuelson.) In the first week of 1969, the Dow Jones Industrial Average stood at 16.7 times its estimated 1968 earnings. But that 16.7 was modest compared with the prices of many individual issues. Many stocks were selling in the over-the-counter markets, on the American Exchange and even on the New York Stock Exchange at 40, 50, or 60 times earnings.

With dour economic comments coming from so many reputable and respected men, the market became less exuberant. In the first quarter of 1969, it slid gently backward from its

75

December 1968 highs. It backed and filled, but the general pattern tended to be lower. Conglomerates began to lose their glamorous look.

Looking back on the markets of late 1968 and early 1969, the signs of the times seem easy to read. But all was not so clear at the time. The signs were obfuscated by some erratic market behavior: for five successive weeks in 1969 the market staged what appeared to be a convincing rally, rising to a recovery top of 952.70 for the Dow—not far below the December 1968 peak. But the stocks that were influencing the averages were the blue chips. Many others were slipping in a virtually continuous downward line.

On February 25, 1969, reality asserted itself. The averages fell below 900 for the first time since August 30, 1968. The fundamental factors that we have been discussing were obviously behind the decline, which soon began to take on alarming overtones. The immediate catalyst was an external event—a statement by the man who was then still Chairman of the Federal Reserve System, William McChesney Martin.*

The chapter of history begun by Martin's remarks is very revealing. Above all else, it shows the complex interplay between the stock market, the bond market, money rates and the money supply. It is as though the four fields were wired together, with electric impulses from one touching off responses in the others—but only after an indeterminate and irregular time lag. Generally, the prime mover is the money supply and the interest rates which depend upon it. However, the bond market does not move in immediate and direct correlation with movements in the money stock. Nor does the stock market respond predictably to movements in the bond market. What takes place is an elaborate point-counterpoint, with each episode of price movement subject to analysis and understanding after it has taken place, but never truly predictable in advance. The delicate nature of the interrelationships reinforces my belief that the best men dealing in bonds are those with an intuitive, gut feeling for the marketplace—a sense developed by experience, but only possessed by those who have more than experience: a real flair for the deal. I

---

* This was by no means the first time that Martin's statements had a dramatic effect on the stock market. Ten months before, on April 20, 1968, he had made comments about the bull market then rampant and compared some of its movements to those that occurred in 1931. There was an immediate, although brief, sag in what came to be known as "Martin's Market."

can recall no time in recent history when that kind of flair was so important.

Martin was testifying before a Congressional committee—specifically, the Joint Economic Committee, which holds annual hearings on the state of the economy, drawing testimony from various experts on the field of finance—when he rocked the Street with his comments. Martin indicated to the committee, which is composed of some of Capitol Hill's most financially sophisticated legislators, that interest rates throughout 1969 would remain at the then-current levels—and they were already close to their highest in history. Martin made it emphatically clear that the Federal Reserve Board looked on inflation as public enemy No. 1. He also forcefully drove home the Fed's resolve to fight that enemy, perhaps by increasing the discount rate (**G**) or boosting reserve requirements (**G**) for member banks. Martin said the Federal Reserve Board "meant business" about keeping credit tight all year to cool the economy. He added that he hoped the Government could achieve "disinflation"—reducing the rate of price increases—without actually causing "deflation," a downturn in business that reduces prices. But the Fed Chairman cautioned that "this has never been done before too successfully." Policy makers, he concluded, "have to take some risks."

While the liquidity position of banks as a group was not quite as strapped as it had been in the fall of 1966, he said, "the ability and willingness of banks to help finance credit-based spending is clearly becoming more and more limited." In an unprecedented disclosure of information that had previously been kept a closely guarded secret, Martin included in his testimony the 1969 forecasts of the Board's staff of economists. The forecasts stressed that commercial banks would probably have to continue "rationing" credit to their customers to hold the expansion below the previous year's level.

An immediate drop in prices on the stock market followed Martin's very blunt appraisal. But, in accordance with the dictum that "nothing is simple in finance," the drop was not continuous. The market moved in a sawtooth pattern, down and up, down and up, indecisively. Stock prices continued to be influenced by all kinds of minor events. As though to demonstrate its eccentric nature, the market began to recover quite quickly from the shock of Martin's remarks to the Congress. That rally did not exhaust itself until May 1969, by which time the Dow Jones had hit 963, which put it only 21 points or so below its all-time peak.

But at that juncture, the scent of inflation was in the air, and it became more and more obvious that the investing public did not like the smell. The old theory that inflation drives up stock prices was about to be blasted to bits. Investors simply did not believe that the administration was sufficiently serious about its efforts to bring inflation under control, or that the efforts were likely to be successful. Neither did investors believe enough in Milton Friedman's theories to accept the fact that the Federal Reserve Board could accomplish a cooling of inflation by the tools Martin had indicated he would use.

In another interplay of forces, a report from the Department of Commerce that the wholesale price index had advanced once again had a heavy impact. The wholesale price index had been rising in the previous six months at an annual rate of 4.5%, and that was high enough to alarm investors. Now it was still advancing; and a series of large wage settlements were made with annual percentage increases that seemed incredible to the average non-union man, even those earning high salaries. Such settlements continued through 1971, with aluminum workers, steel workers, and others getting big increases—until checked by the 90-day freeze that began in August.

The interrelationship of stock prices and interest rates was never clearer than in 1969. On May 14 the Dow Jones industrials stood at 968.85. And interest rates were continuing their assault on Everest. Once-cheap Eurodollars, described in the previous chapter, were commanding an interest rate of 9 1/4%. In view of the rates it offered, the Eurodollar market became a magnet for dollars everywhere else in the world. Between January 1, 1969, and May 14, 1969, the total number of dollars making up the Eurodollar pool rose by about 50%, to almost $3.2-billion. This, in some measure, explained a loss of some $7-billion in certificates of deposit issued by commercial banks. (Recognizing the high rates, the Bank of England increased its rate of discount from 7% to 8% to divert an outflow of the pound sterling.)

Higher rates began to beat the stock market down, something like a man driving piles with a hammer. In June the New York call money rate (**G**) went up from 7.5% to 8.5%. By the end of June the stock market was down to around 870. Everything was in flux—only the Fed at that time remained unmoved. Indeed, the Fed proposed at this point that commercial banks be required to hold reserves (**G**) against their Eurodollar liabilities. What this meant, in effect, was that the obligations in the Eurodollar market of the subsidiaries of American banks abroad were reduced by the level of reserves imposed by the Fed—in this case, by 10%. The regulation went into effect in October 1969. Its result was to put a further pinch on the banks, which were already squealing about the increasingly tight situation in which they found themselves.

Inevitably, some voices were raised in protest against the economic policies that had been set in motion. Walter Heller, Chairman of the Council of Economic Advisers under Presidents Kennedy and Johnson, urged President Nixon to impose wage and price controls as a more expedient way to control inflation. He was saying, in effect, that the classic anti-inflationary antidote of tight money would either be ineffective or would be so slow to take effect that the cost to the country would be excessive. A major public debate on the matter of wage and price controls ensued; it culminated with the August decrees. In its December 1969 issue the Chase Manhattan Bank publication decried "the surprising amount of business sentiment for wage and price controls." This attitude, said the banks, flew in the face of overwhelming evidence that such controls are "economically debilitating and, for both political and economic reasons, will not control inflation." In June 1970 the First National City Bank, in its *Monthly Economic Letter,* conceded that the motives of those who would impose controls were "undoubtedly of the highest." But, it added, if the United States had learned anything from recent history, it was the "amount of damage to the social fabric" that could result from the adoption of controls. "At best," the letter continued, "formal systems of controls may affect the timing of price increases, as probably occurred in the United States during World War II. But in the end, the overly expansive monetary policy that is at the root of inflation will have its way with prices."

The article went on to say that recourse to controls was "almost certain to increase tensions in society rather than reduce them. Most important, controls only serve to obfuscate the real causes of inflation. If there is inflation, government monetary and fiscal authorities are responsible and must take the corrective action, if it is to be stopped. Controls are a tranquilizer at best, dispensed to dull the symptoms of the inflationary disease rather than eliminate the cause." Since then, of course, controls have been clamped on to an American peacetime economy for the first time in history. Cutbank's predictions as yet have been neither proved nor disproved. The difficulty of administering controls evenhandedly is clear; that they will increase social tension is possible—especially as regards relationships between labor and other groups—but not certain.

Arthur Burns, economic counselor to President Nixon at the time, bore the brunt of the Administration's argument. Responding to the cries of Heller and others, he insisted that no controls would be imposed by the Administration. He admitted that efforts to fight inflation could lead to more unemployment, which indeed they did, but he held fast to the theory that wage and price controls would mean more distortions and ultimately more suffering. He recommended hanging tough. Later Burns was to change his mind as the stubborn economy refused to respond; as Chairman of the Fed, he fought for some form of controls and Government jawboning, and eventually, on August 15 after a long weekend at Camp David, he had his way. He is a pragmatic man.

At the time, though, the Fed under Martin felt the weight of Burns' logic. It intensified its tight money policies. J. L. Robertson, one of the members of the Federal Reserve Board, warned commercial banks not to make any move which had the effect of circumventing the objectives being sought by the Fed. Specifically, Robertson referred to the sale of commercial paper by one-bank holding companies. Banks themselves did and still do face legal hurdles that make it difficult for them to compete in issuance of commercial paper. But a company that owns a bank might do so; indeed, one-bank holding companies had raised $1.2-billion by the issuance of commercial paper. The banks were doing this in an effort to offset the runoff in certificates of deposit. But the issuance of commercial paper was, in fact, having the effect that Robertson was worried about, and he regarded the issuance as little more than a corporate dodge. The practice ceased with his fiat.

With the money supply thus becoming tighter and with interest rates continuing to rise, new blows were struck at the stock market. During July, the market came down to a low of 802 on the Dow Jones Industrials. Again to demonstrate that no correlation is clear and continuous, the market rallied slightly during August, a time when rallies are almost traditional, but in September the brief period of exuberance was over. William McChesney Martin let in a ray of hope when he remarked that "we may be getting to the end of this period of very high interest rates," but that was only a flicker and it was snuffed out quickly with Martin's own disclaimer, added immediately, that he was not making a forecast.

The bond market obviously agreed that he was not. A $150-million Southwestern Bell Telephone Company issue was offered to investors at 8.14%, the first time a Aaa corporate security provided lenders with a yield above 8%. Municipal issues—issues sold by states, cities and municipalities—were by no means exempt from the forces at work. New York State came to market with an $84-million issue and had to pay from 4.5% to 6.5% to lenders, depending upon the time to maturity. The longer the duration of a bond, the higher the interest rate, generally speaking. This rate, in view of the fact that it offered a tax-free return, was surprisingly high—indeed the highest that New York State had had to pay for money in 40 years. So neither the security of Aaa nor the lure of tax-exempt interest was sufficiently strong to bring rates down.

While the key elements in this equation were financial, the situation—already complicated and unpredictable enough—was further tangled by outside influences. The stock market's rally in October was based in part on one of the elements we have been considering—the hope of an easing of the monetary crunch. But it was brought on less by that hope than by news from Vietnam indicating the war might shortly come to an end. Economic forecasts, growing more optimistic, also provided the market with a spur. Milton Friedman, always influential and voluble, had a long discussion with newsmen during which he remarked that the Federal Reserve might already have begun to ease its tight money policies, even though the statistics were not yet in hand to bear him out.

This kind of prescience was weighed with particular care by the experts. Henry Wallich, a professor of economics at Yale and a senior economic adviser to the Secretary of the Treasury, added his voice to Friedman's, saying that 1970 might "bring a significant lessening to the rate of inflation." He also indicated that the economy was "showing a sign of a slowdown," and in that fevered atmosphere any talk of cooling by policy makers was welcome. Similar comments came from Tilford Gaines, vice president and economist of New York's Manufacturers Hanover Trust Co., who said that a statistically measurable recession might already have begun, or, if it had not, it would surely develop within the next year.

Yet such encouragement could not endure without the sequel of hard evidence. So the paradox of good news led the stock market downward. The brief rally in the stock market peaked out on November 10 at 863, and by early December had dropped below 800. This was the lowest level the stock market had reached since January 1967, almost three years earlier. Meanwhile, the bond market continued to sag.

Under certain conditions one day of decline encourages a further decline on succeeding days. When the Dow Jones dropped below 800, technicians, those who analyze the market through charts and other measures of market behavior and market psychology, lost confidence in the sturdiness of what had been regarded as a floor under prices. With 800 reached, there seemed no reason why 750 would be far behind.

And from the administration, no cheerful wind blew. The running fire of comment that inflation must be beaten continued, but emphasis fell on how hard the job would be. The President himself, reinforcing the statements of his subordinates, told a gathering of nearly 2,000 businessmen that we were surely in for a "painful" period of very slow growth. He added that the economy would not be allowed to rebound from that slow growth in jumps as great as the ones that had marked the recent past. Indeed, the President said, "we intend to continue our present policies until we are sure that they will work." Governor Maisel of the Federal Reserve System supported the President's judgment, saying the actions already taken would be sure to slacken demand over the next several quarters. Slackened demand, of course, would help to moderate the rate of rising prices, which, in turn, would improve the foreign trade balance. But it also meant a slowdown for the economy as a whole, and smaller profits for corporations.

If this all sounds as though the trends were unmistakable and as easy to read as the falling leaves in October, let me point out the conflicting evidence that was also operating. One of the most important elements in consideration of inflation is the outlook for expenditures by business on plant and equipment. Such investment tends to have a dual and somewhat contradictory effect. Companies spending money on new plant and equipment would be adding to inflationary pressures; but once in place the new and more efficient plant and equipment could be expected to turn out products with a lower labor-cost content. Thus spending on new plant and equipment would eventually lead to higher productivity and reduce inflationary pressures.

With labor costs rising, businessmen were stepping up expenditures for new plant and equipment. A Commerce Department survey made late in 1969 indicated that plant and equipment spending in the first quarter of 1970 would run at an annual rate of $76.85-billion, a $3.6-billion increase over the estimated rate in the last quarter of 1969. Total spending for plant and equipment in the second quarter of 1970 was expected to rise by $1.4-billion over the first quarter.

None of this seemed to jibe with all of the talk about a recession and slowdown. But the Commerce Department's figures were only estimates, and, indeed, turned out to be too optimistic. With industry operating at only 73% of capacity, well below the most efficient level, spending plans were presently cut back. In 1971 new investment in plant and equipment rose only 2.1% over 1970's $79.7-billion, and that rise, of course is more than accounted for by inflation. The importance of this sector of the economy is considerable. It normally accounts for close to 10% of the Gross National Product.

The year 1969 closed with the prime interest rate at 8 1/2%. The stocks composing the Dow Jones Industrial Average were selling at 14 times their 12-month earnings, the equivalent of the low ratio that pertained at the bottom of the 1966 decline, and considerably below the earnings ratio during the 1962 bear market. So, not only were stocks declining, but the earnings multiple (**G**) by which they are valued was also dropping—a kind of double whammy, since a decrease in earnings accompanied by a decrease in the earnings ratio leads to an accelerated decline in stock prices.

As year-end neared, the two axes were chopping away steadily. The Fed and the Administration were insisting that inflation had to be beaten. They were saying, with absolute truth, that the inflationary psychology was deep-seated and that it would be a long time before inflation would take its claws out of the economy's flesh. And, matching chop for chop, the stock market was coming down, as interest rates rose.

Political decisions continued to have their influence. On October 17, 1969, President Nixon had appointed Arthur Burns to be the new Chairman of the Federal Reserve Board, succeeding William McChesney Martin Jr., who had been chairman for 19 years.* No one knew whether Burns would seek to change the course the Fed had been following. Those who hoped for a change said they expected one, while those who hoped things would remain the same argued that the appointment represented continuity rather than a break from the status quo. No one could foresee the unusual, wide-swinging relationship that finally developed between Nixon and Burns— first the reports that all was harmonious between them, then an apparent break over the management of the economy, and later still, restoration of amity with the President's August 1971 actions.

Burns himself was closemouthed in public following his appointment. On February 7 he appeared before the House Banking and Currency Committee. Pipe-smoking, friendly and cooperative, he declined to give any indication about when the Fed would reverse its highly restrictive credit policy, which by then had been in effect for 14 months. The new Fed Chairman did pledge "to do everything in my power to help this country prevent a recession." But he added, not without a certain element of paradox, that for the near term "it would be vital to preserve the taut fiscal position outlined in the Administration's pledges." He insisted that the economy must cool before interest rates could be lowered. At the same time he refused to support a suggestion that taxes should be raised to speed up the braking of the economy and thus to hasten a decline in the rate of inflation. With the canniness that has long been characteristic of him, he left his options open.

Widespread public approval followed Burns' testimony, both in Congress and among the business community. But the stubborn markets were not encouraged. By February 1970 the stock market had dropped below 769.93—another floor, built on December 17, 1969. Once through the floor, the market started down the cellar stairs.

The bond market also made its depressing contributions. In the last week of January two leading corporations, American Telephone & Telegraph and Chrysler, announced large offer-

---

* During that time Martin had been encrusted with honors and also badgered by opponents, particularly Congressman Wright Patman, Chairman of the House Banking and Currency Committee. Patman, an old-fashioned Texas populist, thought Martin's monetary policies had been far too restrictive, and he had publicly tangled with Martin on several occasions. Yet Martin had had a distinguished career in finance. In 1938, at the age of 32, he became the first paid president of the New York Stock Exchange. In 1971 he was called back by the Stock Exchange to do a far-ranging study on Exchange procedures.

ings of new debt securities. AT&T offered 8 3/4 percent, 30-year debentures, totaling $1.5-billion, and another $1.5-billion in bonds and warrants. Totaling $3-billion all together, it was the largest issue in corporate history. Chrysler offered $200-million in new debt securities—half of it on an 8 3/4 percent note and the other half on a 8 7/8 percent sinking fund debenture.

Then that difficult and delicate lock-step between interest rates and the stock market, at times obscure and indirect, emerged very clearly. As we've seen, throughout December and January, as the command at the Fed had shifted from Martin to Burns, Open Market Committee operations remained moderate. But after January 15 a more expansive policy gradually became evident. Gradual rather than expansive is the controlling word here. In its widely read and influential bank letter, the First National City Bank noted that in the November just past the Fed had pumped more reserves into the banking system than usual for that time of year—a much noticed and much analyzed break in the clouds.

This increase in reserves was the beginning of the process that eventually led the economy out of the recession of 1969–1970. But it took a long time for the economy to begin to come out of its doldrums; during the lag, the stock market continued on its precipitous slide, heading toward its dramatic selling climax in the week of May 26. Yields on bonds moved higher still, reaching a peak of 9.5% in June 1970 when Union Light Heat and Power, an Aa-rated utility, sold $10-million in bonds at that rate.

I cannot leave this period of history without discussing a distinguished maverick of the money market. John R. Bunting Jr., president of the First Pennsylvania Banking & Trust Co., Philadelphia's largest bank with $3-billion in assets, has a penchant for shaking up staid Philadelphia (and indeed national) banking circles. (His bank also has a fine earnings record.) Waves of shock passed through the oak-paneled boardrooms of the Quaker City when he revealed that he was considering the possibility of turning over a third of his bank's 24 directorships to consumer representatives, young adults, employees, blacks, poor persons and perhaps even militant feminists. Bunting also spoke of establishing a perpetual seat for a youth on the board of directors. The seat would have to be vacated when the holder reached the ripe old age of 26. He envisioned a poor man's seat, which would be held only so long as its occupant earned less than $10,000 a year.

To his credit, Bunting was among the first to lower the traditional barricades in banking against hiring blacks on all management levels. He advanced more than $5-million in loans to budding black businessmen—more than all other Philadelphia banks combined. He also bucked the tide by refusing to market a bank credit card, a popular new medium for many banks. Similarly, Bunting broke with tradition by issuing $20-million in capital notes in denominations as small as $100, bearing an interest rate of 7 1/4%—far higher than any obtainable from regular savings accounts.

Friends of Bunting take pleasure in telling anecdotes about him. They relate that once when asked where he went to school, he replied, "Temple O."

"Temple O.? You mean Temple U., don't you?"

"No, I mean Temple O. You see, when my friends are asked where they went to school, their reply is usually Pennsylvania, Yale, Harvard, or Princeton. There are smiles and nods of approval. Then they ask me, and when I reply 'Temple,' they say, 'Oh.'"

In recent years Bunting's First Pennsylvania Banking & Trust Co. has frequently been a leader in cutting or raising its prime rate, moves once traditionally reserved for one of the big New York banks. In many instances the other banks eventually followed. On September 14, 1970, First Pennsylvania lowered its prime rate from 8% to 7 1/2%. Within 10 days the nation's other banks did the same, many of them reluctantly. And on January 4, 1971, Bunting's bank again led in lowering the prime rate, this time from 6 3/4% to 6 1/2%. The big New York and California banks huffily proclaimed that First Pennsylvania's action was "premature," but in three days they all followed. Five months later First Pennsylvania took the lead again, increasing its prime rate on this occasion from 5 1/2% to 5 3/4%. This time the big bankers moved their rates 1/4 point beyond the 5 3/4% rate Bunting had set.

• • •

In a golf game you may be going along two or three up on your opponent and feeling pretty good. But the concurrence of one or two incidents can change all that with lightning speed. You miss a shot, you get an unlucky bounce, and then your opponent suddenly sinks a long one. From your point of view it all starts to go sour—but from his point of view, everything is looking up. As is pretty clear from what I have already related, Wall Street was not doing particularly well as the spring of 1970 approached. Events external to the Street, and those concerning the economy at large, as I've reviewed, were all depressing prices. And of great importance was another element thus far barely touched on: corporate profits.

The bad news was both internal and external. Some giant corporations reported large losses for the first quarter of 1970. Chrysler and TWA announced deficits of $29.4-million and $39.7-million respectively. Penn Central, the nation's largest railroad, also reported a resounding $62.7-million loss, with the effect on its stock mentioned previously. Soon it was headed down the tracks toward bankruptcy. Of course, analysts had been watching these companies, and the fact that they were going through some tough times was pretty well known. But no one expected their losses to be of this magnitude.

The combined news about Chrysler, TWA and Penn Central jolted Wall Street. Among the more literate circles there—and, despite opinion to the contrary, there are literate people on Wall Street—the Street's state of mind was described at that time as "anomie," meaning "a feeling that there is no bottom." When asked whether the market would soon turn upward again, analysts were apt to reply: "I can't see any reason why it should." I have no doubt that those were perfectly objective and honest analytical judgments, based on what the analysts saw around them, or perhaps it would be more accurate to say saw falling around them. For all of their charts, computers, analytical aids, Wall Street's analysts are human enough to be affected by mood as well as math.

Profits for firms operating within the canyons of the Street itself were also perilously hard hit. For at this time lots of brokerage firms were operating in the red. Some were about to turn belly-up. At the time, few firms on the Street published very much financial data about themselves, although more are now getting the habit. But from what I know, from what I heard at the time, and from what I could sense around me, I would guess that probably all except about a half a dozen firms on the Street —pleasantly enough, Merrill Lynch was among the half dozen —went through months of severe losses of capital about this time. Some had a losing year; some had two losing years.

Everybody, even those in the blue ribbon half-dozen, felt the pinch.

Lots of reasons contributed to these circumstances. The starting point of Wall Street is always volume—the number of shares that changes hands. The operative axiom is worth repeating: for every seller there must be a buyer, and for every buyer a seller. But the affair goes deeper than that, since for us on the Street to be prosperous we need not only to match up buyers and sellers, but we need a fair number of each. At this time, sellers were not getting out unless they had to. And until the market made that dramatic sweep upward following the selling climax of late May 1970, buyers were scarce. Potential buyers and potential sellers spent a lot of time just staring at each other. It seemed as though neither one was ever going to move. The resultant quiet standoff was just the kind of impasse that Wall Street likes least.

This sense of there being no one on the Street even at high noon was particularly disturbing in view of the kind of industry that Wall Street was, or thought it was, until the big bear took over way back in 1964. So members of the New York Stock Exchange decided it would be a good idea to have a look at what the Exchange was likely to become over the next decade. As usual, a study was commissioned, and as usual, it made projections based on the past—just about the only way to make them, I grant. But the trouble with such studies and such projections is that the assumptions, especially the basic one that the past can tell us a good deal about the future, are too often accepted as gospel instead of being taken with a large pinch of skepticism.

To no one's great surprise, the study painted the securities industry as a major growth industry. The technique of extending past performances through the present and into the future made that conclusion inevitable. In the previous bull market of 1960–61, which ended abruptly in 1962, the average daily volume on the New York Stock Exchange was 3- to 4-million shares. But less than five years later, in 1965, the average daily volume was just over 6-million shares. The straight line projection, as generally adhered to by the New York Stock Exchange study, indicated that the average daily volume would be somewhere around 11- or 12-million shares by 1975.

Like all such predictions, this one had the effect of dividing the sympathies and judgments of the people who read it. One camp immediately attacked the study for being much too optimistic, arguing that volume by 1975 would certainly never reach the pinnacles that the study foresaw. This group thought that the biggest pothole ahead on the Street was the prospect that volume might dwindle—not that it would grow. But others thought that the study was, in fact, far too conservative. Their view was that inflation and increasing affluence would cause the number of shareholders to increase, and trading would rise at a more accelerated pace than the study predicted. Folding in all of those considerations, these highside guessers came to the conclusion that by 1975, 13- to 14-million shares a day was a much better estimate.

Neither camp, however, applied a rule of thumb that was once current on the Street, and which I have come to put quite a bit of faith in over the years. It is a rule I have cited to some members of the press in interviews from time to time, but it never got the circulation, or the credence, that I believe it deserves. Simply stated, the rule is that in any given year the highest volume on any one day—that is, the record day of the year—will be twice that of the average daily volume. For example, on a year in which the average daily volume is 5-million shares, the high day will see about 10-million shares traded. If the average daily volume works out to 12-million shares, the high day for the year will be about 24-million.

The rule has held true in 45 of the last 50 years—a very high percentage. If it were applied in the case of that New York Stock Exchange study, the peak day for 1975 would be around 22-million shares. But the estimate of the more optimistic—if that is the right word for those who believed higher volume was coming—was that the Exchange would be seeing occasional 28-million-share days by 1975.

Between the time I first set pen to paper to start this book and the present—the moment of its completion—the whole pattern of the volume of trading in listed securities has been radically altered. Those who believe the Stock Exchange's estimates to be too modest and too conservative, and thus inadequate for future planning, are being proved right. During 1971, average daily volume on the New York Stock Exchange was 15.4-million, far exceeding the expectations of even the most optimistic forecasters. The first quarter was easily the year's most active. A total of 1.1-billion shares changed hands, and average daily volume was 18-million shares per day. In this 90-day period the previous daily record of 21.35-million shares, set in 1968, was broken on nine different occasions, one of them a 28.25-million-share day. And on August 16, 1971, yet another record was set when 31.73-million shares were traded.

Once again the old rule proved accurate. The average daily volume of 15.4-million was roughly half of the peak day of 31.7-million.

This tremendous volume, of course, seems even greater because it came so suddenly after the long dry period of the bear market and its accompanying sparse activity. But the point is that the peak days have already far outrun the ten-year estimates made by the experts only six years ago. Among the more modest conclusions I would draw is that it is time for a new study; while I tend to be skeptical about all studies, they can be useful in helping us to plan for the future. Nonetheless the unpredictable elements, the outside forces and their influences, are so strong that the plans will always have to be subject to quick change.

Some dissection of the components that make up New York Stock Exchange volume can perhaps help to instruct us. By extension, these same components make up the volume on other exchanges. A major factor is the number of shares that are available for sale or purchase through any given exchange. The numbers of shares listed on the New York Stock Exchange has been increasing every year since the end of World War II. At the end of 1950 the 1,057 companies listed on the New York Stock Exchange had a total of 2.35-billion shares outstanding. By 1960 that figure had almost tripled to 6.5-billion shares. By 1965, an additional 50% increase had taken place, and the total number of shares listed was 9.643-billion. By 1970 the number of shares listed on the New York Stock Exchange had surged to 16-billion shares.

Besides the number of shares listed, the turnover ratio is of great significance. The turnover ratio is the number of shares that are actually traded in relation to the average number that are listed—the first given as a percentage of the second. (It should be noted in this connection that the turnover rate for all stocks has no relation to the rate for any single stock.) In 1929, that year which is still so much a point of reference in the mind and heart of Wall Street, the turnover ratio was 119%; in 1928 it was 132%. In short, everybody was selling almost everything to everybody else. But this Indian bead trading could not continue.

By the 1950s and through to the mid-1960s the turnover ratio had settled down to a much lower and more stable rate. In the '50s and early '60s, the rate ranged between 12% and 19%—meaning, you will remember, that 12% (or 19%) of the total shares listed on the Exchange changed hands during the year. Understandably enough, since that long period of 15 years witnessed virtually no change in the turnover rate, the New York Stock Exchange study accepted the ratio thus established as a near-constant. The resultant calculations was essentially quite simple. By 1975 20-billion shares would probably be listed. The turnover ratio for the full year was estimated at 12.5%. Therefore, the average daily volume comes out to 12.5% of 20-billion, divided by the number of working days (approximately 250), or about 10-million shares per day. A schoolboy can understand it. But only a schoolboy could really believe it.

In a way, Wall Street looked on its future in somewhat the same way as the manager of a small plant manufacturing tin cans would. He would figure population growth in the small area he is serving, assume a certain increase in consumption based on past experience and calculate the number of air-filled tin circles he had to make over the next five-year period. A big can company, though, would look at its situation very differently; once you think of yourself as a packager, and the creator of a special package-product relationship, everything gets more complicated and interesting. But many on the Street thought of themselves rather fondly as being engaged in a business that offered slow, steady growth; that, after all, was what the past 10 years had offered. And, again as every school boy who has been to Washington knows, what is past is prologue.

But a vital premise was overlooked.

The premise has been stated this way: all history is the unfolding of miscalculations. The unfolding began in 1967. The average daily volume leaped to 10-million shares, up from 7.5-million shares in 1966. But 1967 turned out to be only the platform from which much, much larger missiles were to be launched. In 1968 average daily volume was almost 13-million shares, and the high day was 21-million shares.

Behind those figures, and in a sense the engine that was driving them upward, was the turnover ratio. In 1966 the turnover ratio was 18%, compared with 16% in 1965. In 1967 it jumped to 22%, an increase of approximately 22%. By 1968 the turnover ratio was 24%, an increase of 10% over 1967. And, with more than 13-billion shares then listed, the increase in the turnover ratio meant an annual increase of 130-million in the number of shares traded.

To most firms on the Street, this upward path looked like

a highway to riches. Particularly in 1967 and early 1968, the Street took on a golden glitter. General (**G**) and limited partners (**G**) were delighted by present and prospective profits. Salesmen—registered representatives (**G**), whose earnings are geared to the volume of business they do— never had it so good and were frank to admit it.* In the back offices new job openings abounded, and raises were being granted with great frequency. Proselytizing among people who work in the operations area, which was for years called "the back office," suddenly became common. This was big news on Wall Street, where the salesman had been king for so long. Profits for Wall Street firms were greater than they had ever been in history. Business was rolling in the front door, being processed, and rolling merrily out the back, with a nice little chunk of it staying behind in the form of increased profits.

With all of this volume, individuals swarmed into the market. In part they were motivated by phrases that Charles E. Merrill, Merrill Lynch's founder, made famous: "bringing Wall Street to Main Street" and "owning a share of American business." The epigrams reflected Merrill Lynch's long-standing philosophy that doing business with a small investor can be profitable to both the investor and the broker. Our firm had its highest profit year in 1967, when we earned $57.6-million, and our second best year in 1968 when we earned $49.1-million. (We have been breaking all records in 1971.) Given the manner in which the New York Stock Exchange raises its revenues (**G**), it experienced a record year in 1968, when there was an excess of $6.9-million in revenues over expenses. In 1968 and 1969 the price of a seat on the Exchange reached $515,000, the highest since 1929—when a record price of $625,000 was paid. Attached to the 1929 price, however, was the right to sell a 25% interest in the membership, which lowered the actual price of the seat without the right to $500,000.

Another onrushing change that stimulated the prosperity of Wall Street firms in the brief golden age of 1967 and 1968 was the increased size and activity of financial institutions. The institutions were enlarging their place in the economy in general, and they were expanding the role they played in the

---

* Merrill Lynch's compensation policy must be differentiated from that of most other firms on the Street. We do not compensate our account executives simply on the amount of business they bring in, but instead apply a formula that considers many elements, including customer satisfaction.

financial planning of individuals as well. Pension funds, mutual funds, insurance companies and other organizations that pooled and invested capital were buying and selling securities at a record clip. Some were conservative in their objectives, some were groping for what became known as "performance"; but most of them were certainly engaged in what seemed like endless rearranging of the funds under their control. Those funds were absolutely huge. The Prudential Insurance Company of America, for example, had $10.6-billion invested in bonds and $1.3-billion in stocks by the end of 1968. AT&T had $7-billion invested through its pension funds.

So, with individuals coming into the market in ever-increasing numbers and with institutions trading briskly and with prices still rising, every prospect pleased in 1968. With entry into the business eased by the absence of high and uniform professional standards, some get-rich-quick operators set up shop, prospered briefly, and added to the general euphoria. This mood was, of course, an essential preliminary to the coming sense of anomie.

With the arrival of anomie, the whole attractive landscape began to alter. Actually, the Wall Street skyline took on a less pleasant cast even before the economy got sick—by early 1969 stock prices had already begun to fall. Thus, the Street is proved a leading economic indicator—a lesson from the past that might help us in the future, providing that we can remember it.

The first manifestation of trouble in the Street's firms came from the paper jam that backed up the flow of transactions. All that business pouring in the front door was not flowing so smoothly out the back; before it got out the back, lots of time went by, and lots of mud was churned up. Pools of paper, figuratively, and I have no doubt in some cases also literally, were all over the floor. Errors and customer complaints began to increase.

The first, knee-jerk response of Wall Street management was to employ more people. The total number of people working on the Street greatly increased during 1967 and 1968. In 1965 over 96,000 people were employed by members of the New York Stock Exchange. Of that total, almost 34,000 were registered representatives—the people who actually handle customer accounts and deal with the public. By 1967 the Exchange family began to look more like a boarding house: 129,000 people were employed, over 42,000 of them registered representatives. Registered representatives, as I've noted, were frequently dependent for their standard of living on the number of shares their customers traded; so that while registered representatives were increasing in numbers, they were also acting as multipliers as they sought new business. In 1968 the growth went on: now 163,000 people were employed, 67,000 more than just three years earlier. Almost 50,000 of them were registered representatives, an increase of 16,000 over 1965.

At the same time, following through on their belief that this new volume could be handled by the addition of people and offices—a correlation that turned out to be grossly over-simplified—firms on the Street were adding retail outlets across the country. In 1965 there were 3,521 branch offices of member firms. By 1968 that number had increased by 20% to 4,278. Later the number of offices was to contract sharply. The following table shows the trend.

Flux in the Firms

End of Year	Number of Member Organizations	Number of Offices	Total Personnel of Exchange Community	Number of Registered Representatives
1965	651	3,521	96,300	33,805
1966	649	3,692	107,000	38,514
1967	647	4,130	129,200	42,423
1968	646	4,278	163,000	49,644
1969	622	4,084	165,000	52,466
1970	572	3,636	149,000	50,787
1971	577	3,400	figures not available	

SOURCE: *New York Stock Exchange Fact Book.*

More people and more offices meant higher costs. As the gross number of employees went up, so did the gross costs to the employing firms. At the same time wage scales and rents were rising, too. More and more volume meant both more and more people and longer and longer hours. Overtime costs skyrocketed, as many firms had people working through the night in efforts to straighten out their tangled operations, left over after a busy day. Wall Street also made a discovery that it should have made years before—that training, experience and intelligence in its operational people were necessary ingredients to orderly procedures. But few firms until then had bothered with the development of proper practices of recruitment and training—even though these basic policies were well established throughout American business. So at a time of excess Wall Street was plagued by a vital shortage of experienced people.

Confronted with shortages of competent help and with volumes of work to do, the various firms on the Street began to proselyte from each other. Just about everyone raided everyone else in order to get the experienced help he needed. Part of the raiding, of course, included an offer of more money. Thus costs galloped ahead as though they would never need to be brought under restraint—as though there would be no tomorrow. Experienced margin clerks, transfer clerks and stock loan clerks began to command wages that neither they nor their employers had ever dreamed of. And the collective health of firms on the Street was not improved a bit as a result of these cannibal practices.

CHAPTER VI

The Troublesome
Stock Certificate

HIGH VOLUME, PAPER JAM, UNCONTROLLED costs, ill-considered expansion, and behind all of that, rising stock prices and excessive investment of many firms' capital in common stock because of the prevailing exuberance about the future—all of these streams were bound to have their confluence. If anyone had bothered to listen, they could have easily heard the sound of the cataracts ahead. But generally nobody wanted to talk about that. As John Brooks has pointed out in *Once in Golconda,* belief in Golconda—a mythical city of easy enrichment—was widespread among the faithful.

The earliest sign that the leaders of the brokerage business were at last able to hear the roar downstream came in quite a subtle way. Over lunch tables and in casual conversations I began to notice that more and more attention was being given to the "breakeven point." In industrial terms, of course, that means the number of widgets that you have to make and sell at a given price before you can be sure you will not lose money. This is only superficially an easy concept, since complicated cost calculations, capacities, distribution facilities and a host of other considerations must go into a truly sophisticated calculation. Around Wall Street, however, everybody believed or talked as though he believed that the breakeven point could easily be determined. At that time the gossip—it was really little more than that—was setting the breakeven point very high.

Conveniently overlooked was another little-understood but highly relevant Wall Street axiom. In 1965, a good year for illustrative purposes, the break-even point was considered to be 4.8-million shares of average daily volume on the New York Stock Exchange. In this case 1965 illustrates beautifully the rule I am about to expound, since the year before

96

the average daily volume was 4.9-million shares. Now in the course of 1965 average daily volume jumped substantially, rising to 6.2-million shares. The theoretical break-even point moved up in tandem. In 1966 the break-even point was generally accepted as being around 5.9-million shares daily. And so it went. In 1966 volume averaged 7.5-million shares a day, and by 1967 the experts were putting the break-even point at 7.2-million shares. By 1969, following a year in which the average daily volume was 13-million shares, the break-even point was commonly believed to be 12-million shares.

So you see Regan's Rule of Thumb. The break-even point came to be closely related to whatever last year's average daily volume happened to be. It is as though General Motors were to decide that it could not make money this year unless it sold more Chevrolets than it did last year. Of course, GM *wants* to do that. Often it succeeds in doing it. But it doesn't *have* to do it to be profitable.

On the whole, such a judgment about a break-even point adds up to a sad commentary on the naïveté of much of Wall Street's management. Any student of business knows that costs must and can be controlled, and may even be reduced. Costs can be broken down into components and analyzed, and the growth of the larger and more significant components can often be checked by introduction of new procedures or technology. But it suited the Street at the time to take this somewhat fatalistic attitude—to propound the syllogism that in order to be profitable we need X, and without X, we cannot be profitable.

This propensity of the Street to shrug its shoulders and mutter "Kismet" reveals a great gap between the way Wall Street talked and the way it operated. The Street is at the heart of American capitalism; yet it is retrograde in its understanding and application of some of capitalism's most important concepts. This has become a favorite theme of mine in public addresses; many of the Street's present proclivities will have to change before I give up the theme.

Overlooked in the notion of a "break-even point" is the crucial matter of the mix of the business. Few firms on the Street are pure brokers; that is, few are dependent entirely for their income on the commissions they receive from conducting sales and purchases for their customers. Almost every firm engages in more varied activities. The mix of cost therefore varies with each firm, a fact not yet generally well understood, although likely to gain currency as more brokerage houses sell stock to the public and subject themselves to the scrutiny of security analysts. Some firms do a large commission business, but also have a substantial amount of income from commodities trading. Others may get significant revenues from underwriting, the sale of Government bonds, investment advisory services or the sale of mutual funds. Every one has various points of strength and points of weakness, which will vary as economic and market conditions change. They will also vary as radical reform, which I'll discuss in a later chapter, gradually overtakes the Street.

So the prevailing concept of the break-even point tended to ignore the internal characteristics of each firm. It also overlooked the matter of efficiency and management. A firm might make a lot of money on its New York Stock Exchange business and lose it all somewhere else—or vice versa. Its overall profitability depends on the proper management of its mix, which alone can make a firm profitable. In reality, there is no simple, mythical graph of the volume of transactions below which a firm *must* lose money. But the concept then was much too easily accepted, and is still given more credence than it deserves. The talk about breaking even, however, was an accurate indicator in one respect—it pointed the way straight to trouble. If the community genuinely believed that it could remain profitable only from enormous increases in volume from year to year, something was seriously wrong.

The attention to the dimension of volume distracted attention from the vital fact that in those halcyon years volume was' not being processed properly. Confusion was growing and costs were going beyond control.

Back office operations on Wall Street are something of a mystery to outsiders. Few people who are not in the industry understand the true importance of efficiency on the Street; if it deteriorates far enough, the whole economy could be brought to a halt. In one of his discussions of the nature of a modern economy John Maynard Keynes, even though his definitions were not the same as ours, pointed straight to the soft spot. It was the interrelationship between savings, by which he also meant profits, and investment—the funnel through which money must flow from individuals and financial institutions to the corporations making capital investments. Leaks or clogs in the funnel can be enormously damaging to the operation of the entire economy. And the funnel, or a very long passage of it at least, is Wall Street. Serious foul-ups there can affect investor confidence, slowing the flow of money from savings into investment. Thus the way the sale and purchase of a security is handled—and the price which is charged for handling it, a topic that I shall discuss later—has far-ranging significance not apparent at first glance.

The mechanics of the whole trading process are, therefore, worth understanding. The process begins when an individual tells his account executive to buy, for example, 200 shares of General Motors on the New York Stock Exchange. The account executive transmits that order over his brokerage firm's wires to the floor of the Exchange. There the representative of the firm, called a floor broker (**G**), goes to that point on the Exchange's floor—a sprawling gymnasium with trading areas totaling 29,364 square feet—where GM is traded and bids for 200 shares. Let us assume that he meets at that post another broker who has been instructed by his client to sell 200 shares of GM. The two brokers get together and strike a bargain on price. Once that has been done, reports of the transaction are sent through each broker's wire system to their respective clients. One client is told that he has bought 200 shares of GM; the other is told that he has sold 200 shares; the price, plus a commission for the brokerage function, is reported to both of them.

But that is really only the beginning. The client who made the purchase wants evidence of it. To the sorrow of all brokerage houses and to the disaster of some, that evidence is a stock certificate.* The customer may either want to take

* The world's oldest known stock certificate still in existence is a Swedish document dated June 16, 1288. Written in medieval Latin, the certificate is made of parchment and relates that Bishop Peter Elofsson acquired a 1/8 share in Stora Kopperberg (Great Copper Mountain). Although the mountain's copper is now exhausted, it is still yielding other metals. Stora Kopperberg is today one of Sweden's largest employers, producing pulp, steel, electric power, forest and farm products.

The development of the stock certificate is often synonymous with the development of the crafts of printing and engraving securities. The complicated swirls, stripes, rosettes, borders, lines and geometric patterns that adorn all stock certificates are intended to foil the counterfeiter.

So, too, are the delicate tones, which are almost impossible for forgers to duplicate accurately. Portraits of human figures appear on stock certificates for the same reason. In 1874, following a period when there was a good deal of counterfeit certificates and certificates altered from smaller to larger denominations, the New York Stock Exchange required that all certificates be engraved by bank note engraving companies. The Exchange recommended that 100-share certificates "should have the denomination conspicuously engraved thereon and that certificates of lesser denominations should be of a different style and color." American Bank Note Company, which was founded in 1795, is generally regarded as the United States' biggest security-printing company.

possession of that certificate himself, or he may leave it with his broker, but in either case the certificate stands as evidence of ownership. In short, the buying broker has to arrange to get the stock from the selling broker, and there is nothing at all simple about doing that.

As we have seen, hundreds of thousands of transactions take place every day. On August 16, 1971—the day the New York Stock Exchange made a new record for volume on a single day—there were 68,400 transactions on that Exchange alone. There were 60,600 round-lot sales, which were printed on the tape that day, and 7,766 odd-lot transactions and opening transactions, which are not printed on the tape individually.

To complete the trade, the broker representing the seller first must get the stock certificate from his customer. He then sends it to what is called a transfer agent, where the stock is transferred out of his client's name. In that way, the corporation in which the investment was made knows that this particular investor is no longer a holder of the corporation's stock. At the same time the buying broker also gets in touch with the transfer agent and tells him into whose name the stock should be transferred, but this is done only after the customer has paid for the stock. The regulations of the New York Stock Exchange normally allow five business days for this exchange to be completed.

In the course of these days both brokers are heavily laden with responsibilities. The broker representing the seller must deliver the 200 shares—getting them from the seller eventually, of course. But the broker must deliver them even if the customer is late in presenting them to him. If the selling broker cannot deliver the very same shares sold by his client, he has to deliver an equivalent number; like money, stock is thought of as being fungible—that is, interchangeable. Obviously, the selling broker has to get the shares somewhere, using his own capital if necessary. As for the buying broker, he has to get the money from his client to cover the purchase. Otherwise, he cannot begin the process of transferring the stock to his client's name. If a client is late in paying, the whole procedure is certain to be slowed.

Under the rules of the New York Stock Exchange, delays by the customer in coming up with money or certificates are his broker's problem. The brokers themselves must make their settlement after five business days have elapsed, regardless of their relationship with their customers. If the buying broker does not have his client's money, he has to put up his own. If the selling broker does not have his client's stock, he has to get that stock somewhere and put it in the hands of the buying broker on time. The Federal Reserve Board also insists on this prompt settlement.

Often, the broker representing the seller will borrow stock for this purpose. A current misunderstanding has it that to do this, the broker can use just about any stock within his grasp. *Nothing could be further from the truth.* No broker is legally allowed to make use of the fully paid-for securities that he is holding for a customer. Such fully paid-for securities are segregated. It is a Federal offense to misuse them.*

All securities held by a New York Stock Exchange member firm are carefully checked twice a year by two outside auditors, the examiners for the New York Stock Exchange and an auditor from a public accounting firm. The auditors make surprise visits to each member firm at different times of the year for the purpose of reviewing its books and counting the stock in its custody. The accountants do not announce their arrival—they simply appear. And the first place they go is down to the vaults, where the long and tedious process of counting all securities by hand is carried out. The quantity of securities counted is then checked with the records, to make sure that the two quantities agree.

Although he is forbidden to use his customers' segregated and

---

* Probably the most publicized case involving the misuse of securities was that of Richard Whitney, President of the New York Stock Exchange from 1930 to 1935, who, in March 1938, was convicted of two separate indictments of grand larceny for appropriating to his own use securities entrusted to him in a fiduciary capacity. Whitney pleaded guilty to both charges and was sentenced to five to ten years in Sing Sing.

According to the SEC report on the case, Richard Whitney & Company, a limited copartnership, had "conducted its business as a member firm on the New York Stock Exchange while insolvent." It was further disclosed that as far back as 1926 Whitney had misappropriated a customer's securities entrusted to his care, and that, beginning in 1936, such misappropriations became his regular practice.

"The collapse of Richard Whitney & Company was traced directly to certain outside promotional and speculative ventures of Whitney himself, which had little or no connection with the brokerage business of the firm. These enterprises were uniformly unsuccessful, and the resulting losses far exceeded the profits derived from the firm's brokerage transactions. The result was that the assets of the firm were constantly being drained away in amounts far greater than the firm's capital and earnings could justify. In his desperate need for funds, Whitney borrowed money extensively over a long period of years on one pretense or another from his brother, George, a partner of J. P. Morgan & Company. In addition, he falsified his books and records, misrepresented his financial condition and resorted to the misappropriation of customers' securities."

fully paid-for securities, the selling broker can borrow elsewhere the 200 shares of GM which his delinquent client has
not yet delivered. In a sense, he may also borrow it from
himself. When a customer has a margin account, he is, in
effect, borrowing to buy stock and then pledging the stock
with his broker as collateral. The customers who run margin
accounts sign what is known as a "hypothecation agreement"
(**G**). This agreement gives the broker permission to pledge
the stock of the margin customer to others. This legal and
valid procedure has been going on for over 100 years.

Thus, the selling broker whose customer has failed to turn
in his stock certificate on time can borrow the stock that one
of his other customers has pledged to him as collateral and
turn this stock over to the transfer agent, since the stock is a
fungible commodity. This chain of events can be extended
if the broker who must deliver the stock to the transfer agent
does not have margin accounts or does not find the particular
stock he needs among those accounts. In that event he must
find another broker who does have the stock and can legally
lend it to him.

Thus, there can be many links to the long chain of stock
borrowing. But the essential purpose is to make available to
the buyer what he has bought, and to provide him with
tangible evidence of his ownership as quickly as possible.
Some customers want to keep the certificate in their own possession. Others leave the certificate with their broker, in which case
the customer receives regular statements from the broker, ac-
knowledging that he is holding the certificate.

Located literally on a tight little island, Wall Street is figuratively a tight little island itself. The point is relevant in understanding the Street's dealings with transfer agents. (For a
further discussion of this topic, see Chapter IX.) Almost all
of them are located within a few blocks of each other in the
financial district. In fact, until 1971 the New York Stock
Exchange required that the banks acting as transfer agents
must have their transfer departments or pickup facilities located south of Chambers Street, in lower Manhattan.* This

---

* The exact date when the Chambers Street rule took effect is not
known, because of a gap in the New York Stock Exchange's records.
In 1923 several thousand cartons containing early documents and other
material about stock exchange operations were discovered in the basement of the exchange building at 11 Wall Street. Some 3,000 cartons
were thrown out as having "no current value" to the Exchange at that
time. Out with them, apparently, went the historic origins of the Chambers Street rule.

requirement, aimed at speeding up pickups and deliveries of certificates, also applies to 27 large corporations, including American Telephone & Telegraph, General Motors, General Electric, Bethlehem Steel, U. S. Steel and Union Pacific, which act as their own transfer agents. The banks are paid to carry out this transfer function by the corporations whose stocks are listed on the New York Stock Exchange. But the corporations also have other transfer agents out of town, usually in their home cities and in the other American cities where their stock may also be listed on local stock exchanges —most notably Chicago, San Francisco, Boston and Philadelphia.

Those who defend Wall Street by arguing that it could not have anticipated the great volume of these years can enter a valid argument at this juncture. Commercial banks, after all, are generally considered to be efficient and well-run institutions. Yet the banks which acted as transfer agents were no better equipped to deal with the huge volume of 1967–68 than were the brokerage houses. The transfer departments themselves had not occupied very much of the attention of the banks' top management, since these transfer operations were regarded only as dull routine. But they are also important. As the paper flood began to rise, many banks, like many brokerage houses, found themselves without rowboats.

Before 1967, two to three days usually elapsed between the time the broker sent the stock certificate to the transfer agent and the time when it was returned to him properly registered. Similarly, the purchaser could expect that within a week or 10 days after the settlement of his transaction he would have the stock certificate in his possession. By 1968 such norms were utterly unattainable. The steps of remittance, registration and return took three to four weeks and sometimes longer. Brokers and transfer agents had more work to do than ever before, and they had fewer experienced people to do it. The new clerks who had been rushed in performed about as well as bankers would if they were suddenly put on an automobile assembly line.

At this time a new plural noun—"fails"—became part of the vocabulary of Wall Street followers. Brokers were taking in each other's laundry, but they were not delivering any clean shirts. In other words, they were failing to deliver securities on the fifth business day, and they were therefore often in violation of Rule 64 of the New York Stock Exchange.

The increase in the number of fails created hardships for both brokers and the public. As far as brokers were concerned, their internal relationships were distorted by the growing number of fails—both fails to deliver securities to others and fails to receive them from others. From the standpoint of liquidity and profit, fails to receive should exceed fails to deliver; but the point is that fails can affect brokers on both ends. At a time of very high interest rates and tight money, this shifting tide of fails could keep some brokers afloat, while drowning others. The sums involved were enormous. By December 1968, fails had reached the alarming level of $4.1-billion.

Bad as it was, the jam-up in securities listed on the New York Stock Exchange was surpassed by the delays in the transfer of American Stock Exchange and over-the-counter securities. On July 29, 1968, Congress provided some help by amending the Securities Exchange Act of 1934 to authorize the Federal Reserve Board, which has authority in such matters, to allow margin buying of some securities in the over-the-counter market. Without margin buying, brokers could not lend stock, since they possessed no hypothecated securities; the procedure of borrowing, which supplied at least some grease for the mechanisms of the New York and American exchanges, had been denied to the over-the-counter market. Some of the jams were therefore worse on that market.

Like other service businesses, Wall Street lives or dies by the number of hours it works. Therefore the suggestion that the only way out of the swamp was to reduce trading hours, thereby diminishing volume and giving the back offices more time to work themselves out of their morass, initially got about the same reception as a proposal to supermarket managers that they stay open only from 9:00 A.M. to noon. But finally the New York Stock Exchange had no choice but to restrict the trading periods. In the last half of 1968 the Exchange closed down for one day each week. Later, the system was altered so that the Exchange was opened for five working days, but for only four hours a day instead of the usual five and a half. Yet, even though trading hours had been cut, working hours stretched as brokers attacked the formidable task of bringing the rate of fails under control.

For some, the solution to the fails problem took on aspects beyond practical necessity. Pride, reputation and public confidence were also at stake. Wall Street perhaps more than any other business in America lives under a microscope. It is constantly scrutinized by the Securities and Exchange Commission, other regulatory bodies, the Congress, the press and the public. The tendency to magnify the Street's weaknesses grew as fails became more common. A chorus of criticism began to echo through the Street, although, as is often the case, few of the critics or regulators had any very useful suggestions. My judgment is that the Securities & Exchange Commission missed a rare opportunity for affirmative and helpful regulation at this point, and that both the SEC and the Street are the worse for it today.

The Street floundered desperately under the double weight of internal trouble and external carping. Some firms spent money recklessly to get out from under the crush of paper work. Brokerage houses not only increased their work force, they also laid out huge sums of money in frantic attempts to computerize their operations. Many of these attempts were futile because of the long and tricky steps involved in trading. Many functions could not be readily converted to electronic technology. Since interlocking relationships are at the nub of Wall Street's systems, to be really successful any efforts at computerization had to be made compatible with methods introduced by other institutions—an impossible requirement in a trouble-ridden period.

One of the main reasons for the failure of Goodbody & Co., the fifth largest firm on the Street, was its over-ambitious effort to automate. That ill-fated effort only succeeded in getting Goodbody in deeper trouble. It was trapped in the midst of change: efforts to automate failed, while manual procedure was deserted in anticipation of automation's success. Goodbody & Co. was rescued from bankruptcy's edge when Merrill Lynch agreed to absorb it and its 99 branch offices. Goodbody has now been integrated into our firm.

During the crunch, vast amounts of space were rented to enlarge cages to handle the flow of securities, and to house computers and the people who would feed and care for them. From 1967 to 1970 well over 20-million square feet of office space was built in downtown Manhattan, not including the huge World Trade Center, whose construction was then beginning. Yet for a time nothing seemed to work. Brokerage firms were running three shifts a day, but the volume was still pouring in, and the new, inexperienced employees seemed to be accomplishing little except to move papers from one pile to another.

The Street was caught in a paper blizzard. Paper came in through the doors and windows, and sometimes seemed to come down through cracks in the ceiling and up through the floor as well. Fails were only one of the results. Serious as they are, most fails do get straightened out in time. The resolution of a fail may take weeks or months and may raise the blood pressures of broker, transfer agent and customer, but still, most fails are cleared up eventually, usually within 30 days.

A couple of other complications are graver and even harder to resolve. These are shortages of securities, called "box differences" (G), and the cousin of box differences, "dividend differences" (G). No one will ever know the precise value of missing securities in these days of crisis and chaos. The record keeping was so complex and was so incredibly tangled at the time that the quantities of securities missing simply can't be determined.

But in my judgment there was at least one day in 1969 when, if you had taken all of the securities in all of the vaults in all of the member firms and banks on the Street and counted them, and checked the count against the records, you would have found differences in the range of half a billion dollars. As to how much was stolen, that is a moot point. Investigators for the Senate Permanent Investigating Committee concluded that hundreds of millions of dollars worth of securities were stolen from brokers and banks at this time. Testifying before the committee, I dissented, and continue to dissent in the absence of proof, that thefts really reached so vast a sum. Merrill Lynch's records seem to disprove that any such amount can be attributed to theft. But differences for other reasons may have run that high.

The New York Stock Exchange's surprise audits at the time were turning up some alarming results. On more than one occasion, the auditors found individual firms to be short $10- to $15-million in securities. The firms beset by these huge differences naturally launched intensive searches. But in a number of cases, some involving firms that no longer exist, no amount of this figurative turning of pockets inside out uncovered the missing certificates.

Where they went will remain one of history's mysteries.

It was widely believed that the Mafia had invaded Wall Street. At a sensational hearing of the New York State legislature, a hooded witness testified about how easy it was to steal securities. I do not minimize the gravity of thefts, nor the need for tight security measures on the Street; in fact, I have made concrete proposals in this regard to the Senate Permanent Investigating Committee. But it seems clear to me that box differences resulting from causes other than theft were the main cause of the losses.

Human error played a major role. Under the weight of a heavy work load, a broker representing the buyer and seeking to notify the selling broker might send notice to the wrong broker. Sometimes he might send on the purchased securities; but the buying broker might not find records to show with whom he had made the trade. On the other side, the broker representing the seller might have lost track of whom he had bought from. As a result he might well deny the claim of the legitimate buyer and honor the claim of the wrong one.

Every mistake had a way of multiplying in the back office. A trade that took place in February might well remain unresolved for months. In a surprise audit, let us say in August, the incompleted trade would come to light. But it would be very difficult to reconstruct what had actually happened six months earlier. And in the meantime, dividends were being paid on whatever stock was involved in the transaction. If one dealer expected another to deliver the stock to him, then he would also expect the other broker to deliver the dividends due on the stock. And if the broker representing the seller had had to borrow stock in order to deliver it, then the borrower had to see that any dividends paid while the clock was ticking went to the then-rightful owner. Error compounded error in an endless welter of confusion.

Nothing would please me more than to say that Merrill Lynch sailed serenely through these stormy seas. But unfortunately we did not. Indeed, it would have been impossible for any firm, even one whose operations were perfect—and I must add that Merrill Lynch's operators were better than those of many other houses, but were certainly not perfect—to have functioned smoothly under the prevailing circumstances. Relationships among banks and brokers are such that any substantial difficulties affecting one organization are sure to ensnarl the others. In the brokerage industry, the other guy can make the best in the business look bad.

In the vaults of Merrill Lynch, we held during the time of the big paper crunch about $18-billion worth of securities for our customers. Our box differences and our dividend differences in 1968 and 1969 amounted to $12.6-million—a small percentage, but a large amount of money. Ultimately, we had to make good on all of this out of our earnings. So it was a bitter and costly lesson for us, no less than for others on the

Street harder hit. We have now improved our operations to the point where, even in periods of heavy trading such as December 1971, Merrill Lynch had no significant operational problems. We were able to be a party to the battle and still survive it.

Others were not so fortunate. As they were forced to go into the market to buy stock missing from their vaults—a process known as "buying in"—their profits were wiped out. In some cases the differences ate into the capital, and then ate right through it.

Capital was being eaten up in other ways as well. According to New York Stock Exchange data, clerical and administrative salaries on Wall Street went up in the 10-year period from 1958 to 1968 by 59%. Employees' benefits went up by 57%. The fees charged to brokers by lawyers, auditors, consultants and other service groups (I shall not call them Wall Street's camp followers) went up by 79%. The costs of supplying information from broker to client went up by 87%. And the daily housekeeping expenses, those for rent, heat and light, went up by 91%. It was, of course, a time of rising costs for all of American business, but no sector was hit quite as hard as we were, because so much of the Street's work was done manually. And bear in mind that the figures I have given are increases in unit costs, not increases in total amounts; those total amounts were growing at a much faster rate, since more money was being spent to handle the increment in business.

By late 1969 the Street was to be full of macabre jokes about bodies falling past windows. In point of fact, even when conditions worsened in the following year, there was not much window-hopping. But profits, if not bodies, certainly went out of the window, and in many cases never came back in. Very few member firms on the Street made any profit at all after mid-year 1969. They could not afford to cut their costs because they were obliged to use every means in an effort to locate missing securities and straighten out their records.

So many firms were fully extended when it happened. Choose your own image: lightning struck, an earthquake hit, the impossible happened, a tidal wave came up out of New York Harbor. Volume started to drop—and the long downward sweep, which reached its nadir on those three days in May, was set in motion. In fact, even the steep drop in volume on the New York Stock Exchange was not so great as it was elsewhere. On the New York Stock Exchange volume was off 3.8% in 1969 compared with 1968. Another 3.4% decline occurred during the first quarter of 1970, and 1970 ended with a 1.25% increase over 1969. These early declines, coming at a time when firms were building up, were bad enough. But the decline in volume on the American Exchange and the over-the-counter market was even more damaging.

Member firms do not live by New York Stock Exchange volume alone. They get their nourishment from other markets as well—but these other markets, in fact, were even harder hit than the New York Stock Exchange at the time. On the American Exchange volume was off almost 15% in 1969, 34.5% in the first quarter of 1970 and 36.6% in the second quarter of 1970. For the entire year, it was off 34.5%. In the over-the-counter market, that vast and sprawling market which includes thousands of stocks, the volume declined with even sharper momentum than it did on the American Exchange. There are no precise figures, but good estimates indicate that over-the-counter volume was off between 40% and 50% in the first half of 1970, and off 50% to 60% for the entire year.

Falling volume spelled falling income, of course, and securities firms began casting around for methods to reduce costs. The first item that caught the eye of management was the area where the largest increases had been taking place— the hiring of new people. Despite the urgency of locating and clearing up the differences, the hard decision was made gradually to sweat down the huge clerical force, both by extensive lay-offs and by attrition. By mid-1970 the force was almost 20% lower than at the beginning of 1969. The 10 largest firms belonging to the Association of Stock Exchange Firms (**G**) discharged 23% of their people from mid-1969 to mid-1970. Besides slashing people, the managements of many firms began slashing salaries as well. Cuts of 10% or more were common in many firms. Partners and officers near the top of the pyramid took cuts of 25% or greater. Merrill Lynch was probably the only house on the Street that did not lay people off— indeed, we actually increased our total work force in this period, although only slightly.

Some of these moves obviously succeeded in slicing expenditures. But the sword had two edges. The cuts also laid the groundwork for future trouble, which indeed many firms are still experiencing today. As part of their reduction of expenses, many managements also put an end to their training programs for registered representatives and other employees; at one point at the beginning of 1971, in an industry made up of over 4,600 firms and companies, the only training school in existence on the Street was the one being run by Merrill Lynch.

Almost everywhere except at Merrill Lynch, research services were also cut to the bone: over 600 securities analysts with experience and competence were out looking for work in mid-1970. Those analysts who stayed on were forced to cut back on the source material that goes into their formulation of judgments. Subscriptions to periodicals were canceled, travel was virtually eliminated and computer time was restricted.

Retail outlets were also reduced. A study by the Association of Stock Exchange Firms showed that through the first half of 1970, member firms opened 118 new branch offices—but they closed 211. The new ones were open in the larger cities; those that were closed were in smaller cities. Many offices in those cities were also consolidated into larger units. By these many means, the fat carelessly put on over the years was gradually pared away.

But cost cutting by itself was inadequate unto the needs of the day. Reduction of costs came too late to save many firms from very heavy losses. In total, in 1970 the Wright Associates Reporting Group, a research firm, reported that nine out of 12 leading member firms had suffered losses in the first quarter of 1970. In the 12 months ending January 30, 1970, Bache & Co., the second largest firm on the Street, lost $4.9-million. The firm of F. I. du Pont, Glore Forgan & Co. lost $7.7-million in 1969, and $17.7-million in 1970. Indeed, its troubles went so deep that by April 1971 the firm was skating on the thin ice of bankruptcy. A massive infusion of new capital by Ross Perot, a wealthy Texas businessman and the head of a Dallas-based electronics company, was required to bring Du Pont back to firm ground; Perot became the owner of more than 80% of the equity in the firm as a result. As late as mid-1971, revelations that the true condition of du Pont was worse than anyone knew in April were still coming to light. The most striking revelation of all was the discovery that Du Pont had got so far out of control that no one knew its precise condition. On August 21, the *New York Times* reported that differences of $86-million had thus far been uncovered.

At this writing, volume has picked up on the Street, profits are improving and the market, while not at the levels of 1968, is fairly strong. So it is difficult, even for those of us who lived through it, to recall vividly the atmosphere of the year of the failures. The easiest way to summon back this atmosphere is to review just a few of the more dramatic bankruptcies taking place at the time.

McDonnell & Company. The McDonnell family was very prominent in New York social and financial life for 50 years. Its firm, McDonnell & Company, was very well known, and had just added to its celebrity by taking on as its president Lawrence O'Brien. O'Brien had been a special assistant to President Kennedy, Postmaster General under President Johnson, and he is now for the second time the Chairman of the Democratic National Committee. As matters turned out, it was an unhappy experience for O'Brien, who was president of the firm for only about seven months and left as it began to fail.

Additional capital then was poured into McDonnell, some of whose family members were related to the Fords, but this could not save the firm. Its net worth of $15-million at the end of 1968 had dwindled to $6.175-million a year later. When it closed its doors in March 1970, McDonnell & Co. had lost all of its capital. The New York Stock Exchange put up $8.4-million from its Special Trust Fund to enable customers of McDonnell to get back their securities and cash balances. This example may serve to show the importance of the "box differences" that I was discussing earlier—at one point, they evidently amounted to considerably more than twice the total capital of the firm.

Larry O'Brien, once again Chairman of the Democratic National Committee, came to the Street's attention again some time after his experience at McDonnell. He was reported by the *New York Times* to have approved while absent on vacation in Europe a statement issued by the Committee following the economic decrees issued by President Nixon on August 15, 1971. That statement included the following sentence: "The new economic plan is distinctly Republican in character . . . doing nothing about the windfall profits being accumulated on Wall Street." Members of the New York Stock Exchange now believe that they have finished paying off the debts, including debts to customers, of McDonnell & Co. They all believe and hope that no more levies will be made on their income for that purpose.

Gregory & Sons. Gregory's story is somewhat different from McDonnell's. It too was brought down by box differences. But when it came to liquidating the capital in order to make up these differences, the fact came to light that most of its capital was tied up in "letter stock" **(G)**. Those illiquid assets, if they can be called assets at all, did Gregory no good and its doors closed.

Amott Baker, Blair & Co., White & Co., Dempsey-Tegeler. In every one of these cases, once again, fails, box differences and dividend differences added up to the fatal illness. Blair's troubles were especially acute and far-reaching.

Hayden, Stone also was dragged down by fails and differences and only partially rescued by an infusion of capital from a group of businessmen in Oklahoma. The capital they put in primarily took the form of the common stock of the Four Seasons Nursing Centers. But, in an unhappy combination of circumstances, Four Seasons itself went into bankruptcy. So Hayden, Stone was not relieved by the transfusions.

All these failures involving Wall Street houses took on heightened significance because they might have. damaged many thousands of individual investors, including small ones whose life savings were at stake. For the people who were running the firms to take losses because of a combination of bad luck and their own ineptitude was one thing. But for the public at large to suffer was quite another. That the unsuspecting should thus be gulled was utterly unacceptable.

The Stock Exchange and some of its members are often taken to task for their lack of concern for the public interest; I have fought battles with the Exchange on that ground myself from time to time. But in this case the Exchange community made a noteworthy and entirely successful effort to see that no customers suffered losses as a result of a broker's failure. There was, of course, only one means by which this could be done: to supply money.

Some years before, in late 1963, the Wall Street firm of Ira Haupt & Company failed, following one of the greatest financial swindles ever perpetrated—the $200-million "salad oil" scandal,* involving one Anthony DeAngelis, the American Express Company, and forged warehouse receipts for

---

* In the unfolding of the complicated and dramatic affair, stolen and forged receipts for salad oil were given to Ira Haupt & Co. in payment for loans to a DeAngelis company. Haupt borrowed on them from First National City Bank. At the climax, as Leslie Gould reports in his book *The Manipulators,* "Haupt frantically tried to meet the situation, and arranged a number of 'day loans' with banks and, in violation of Stock Exchange rules, stock on deposit for customers was pledged by the firm for $13.5-million longer term loans. Haupt, unable to meet its commitments, was suspended by the Stock Exchange and later put out of business." It cost Exchange members $9-million to reimburse Haupt's customers for their losses of cash and securities.

more than a billion pounds of nonexistent salad oil. Acting in concert through the Exchange, its members agreed to a levy based on their gross revenues to indemnify the customers of firms that had failed. The levies went into a special fund to be administered by the Exchange. Into this fund the members of the Exchange poured $15-million in cash, and had arranged for another $10-million of credit from a consortium of New York banks in the event that the cash amount should prove inadequate. Virtually every one of the firms that went bankrupt in 1970 constituted some kind of potential liability against this Stock Exchange fund, which, remember, was raised voluntarily by the members of the Exchange. Indeed, at a couple of points in this hectic period, it could be said that the Exchange's governors stretched the uses and the conceptual purposes of the trust fund to the utmost. For example, a loan of $5-million was made to Hayden, Stone out of the fund.

This move, while little publicized or noticed at the time it was made, actually posed some very interesting philosophical questions to those who knew about it. Was Hayden, Stone to pay interest to the member firms for the loan? If not, of course, the loan could be looked on as most unfair in competitive terms—there were few firms on the Street then that could not have used an interest-free $5-million. Or was this really an equity interest? Did it mean that the Exchange was now in effect part owner of a member firm, thus putting the Exchange in competition with one of its own members? These potentially prickly questions have never been answered, and, indeed, the passage of time and the termination of the Exchange's fund have made their answer unnecessary. But many of us who knew about the Hayden, Stone loan were intrigued by this overlay of philosophy.

At the time, though, alarums rather than philosophy filled the air. Cost reductions could not eliminate losses or save collapsing houses. Inevitably, therefore, the Street began to cry for a different kind of relief—the one that appeared both most certain to be effective, and apparently closest at hand, being a price increase.

The commissions paid to brokers for buying or selling stock are fixed by the New York Stock Exchange after approval by the Securities and Exchange Commission. Thus they are mandatory for all brokers. They had not been changed since 1958. Securities firms could with considerable justice, therefore, point to the fact that although the price of everything else had gone up dramatically since 1958, they were still being compensated at the levels of a bygone age.

Of course, arguments against an increase were also raised. Dissenters pointed out that during the periods of high volume in 1967 and 1968, member firms had not pressed for any augmentation of the commission structure, even though their costs were going up. Volume simply overcame the problems of costs in those years. But the Street, so the countervailing rationale ran, had done nothing to increase its efficiency while it was profitable. Now, fallen through its own negligence on hard times, it was proposing to charge the public more—hardly a suggestion that was likely to win much wide sympathy.

But, confronted with what appeared to be a failing industry, and aware of the public dangers involved in the threatened collapse of house after house, the New York Stock Exchange pressed ahead for an increase in rates. In 1968 it had engaged an outside consulting firm called National Economic Research Associates (NERA) to make an extensive study of the need for and nature of increases in the commission rates (**G**). But now the basic issue quickly came down to how much of an increase would be required to make the brokerage industry profitable once again. The fine points of complicated studies took second place in a climate of crisis.

NERA began with the premise—one that I have always found abhorrent in general and erroneous in its particular application to the securities industry—that some fixed rate of return on capital should be determined as a minimum for the industry. In this case, NERA somewhat arbitrarily decided that a 15% return for the securities industry would be justified. With certain monopolies, such as public utilities, rates of return are indeed fixed, and quite properly; for public utilities, the average maximum return allowable on capital is around 8%. NERA's justification for 15% return came down to this: since more risks are taken in the securities industry than in the public utilities industry, a rule of thumb might result in roughly doubling the allowable rate of return.

The correlation didn't really make much sense. Overlooked entirely was the fact that while there is only usually one public utility in any area, most large cities have anywhere from 20 to 50 members of the New York Stock Exchange competing for business. Where there is no monopoly, there ought to be no insurance about return nor limits on it—at least to my mind. NERA also supported its argument for a 15% rate of return by citing the cyclical nature of the brokerage business. As we have seen, volume may go up for two or three years and then down for a year or two, and in NERA's eyes this ebb and flow constituted further evidence for a good rate of return. But such an argument tended to overlook the fact that from 1963 to 1968, the line of climb of volume was virtually unbroken.

The NERA proposals, and the basis that underlay them, touched off a major battle in the Exchange community. Any change in commission rates affects every firm differently, but affects all firms importantly. So the resultant free-for-all was hardly unexpected. Indeed, the Exchange community had gone through a somewhat similar experience in 1958, when it had struggled long and hard to come up with a proposed increase in its commission rates. Then, as in 1970, once past the stage of intramural squabbling the New York Stock Exchange had to face the SEC—which in 1958 promptly ordered the rates cut 10% across-the-board. The precise authority of the SEC to do this is clear: under the Securities Exchange Act of 1934, Section 19 (b), the SEC is authorized to review and, if necessary, to alter or supplement the rules of registered national security exchanges with respect to a broad list of activities, including the "fixing of reasonable rates of commission, interest, listing and other charges." So the SEC has the undisputed power to impose rule changes on the New York Stock Exchange community if it thinks that the community's own regulations, under its self-policing charter, are not consistent with the public welfare. But until 1958 the SEC had left the matter of rates largely in the industry's hands; that year marked its first overt move into rate-making, a role it was to enlarge in 1970 and 1971.

In 1958 Merrill Lynch was a maverick—that is, we opposed the increase in commission rates. And we played the same role in 1970—not, I might add, a role that made the firm as a whole or the members of its top management very popular in the luncheon spots and spas around the Street. Our objection in 1970 was prompted by our belief that the amount of increase that the NERA proposals would have imposed on the individual investor was much too high. In some cases, the rates of the new schedule on small orders would have brought about a cost increase to the individual investor of over 100%. We argued that Wall Street needed "the little people"* and not simply because of the present or future revenues that came

---

* Joseph Mitchell, the author of *McSorley's Wonderful Saloon,* once wrote: "There are no little people. They are as big as you are, whoever you are."

with them. We felt that a capitalistic society must offer all of its people a chance to become capitalists, and that the very steep increases in commissions would inhibit that very desirable social movement. So we fought to hold the commission charged by brokers for the execution of individual orders at an absolute minimum.

The changes that the New York Stock Exchange was proposing went far beyond a commission increase for brokerage done on the floor of that Exchange. Changes in commission rates on the New York Stock Exchange are traditionally followed by comparable changes on all the other exchanges—a once-universal truth that is now for the first time under challenge. But SEC endorsement of the NERA proposals would certainly have brought a like amount of increase to every customer on every exchange everywhere.

Despite the disagreement within the Exchange community, the NERA proposal was unveiled to the SEC by the President and the Chairman of the Board of Governors of the New York Stock Exchange on June 30, 1970. The NERA proposal went off like a firecracker. Merrill Lynch, as I have said, was quick to dissent from the bulk of it. Other firms disagreed with it for an entirely different reason—that the rate of return was not high enough to attract new capital to a cyclical and risk-laden industry. Still others felt that costs had not been adequately considered before the schedule was arrived at. And everybody who was a shareholder—there were 30-million or so around at the time—had an opinion about the increase, and the opinion was unanimous. He did not like it. Letters to Congressmen and letters to the commissioners of the SEC poured in from all over the country. I can testify that Merrill Lynch got its share of them. Shocked and horrified, the SEC held up its ruling on the subject for further study.

Individuals were not the only protestors. On the other end of the scale, large institutions, which had on a provisional basis been granted a volume discount in 1968, also found the new schedule insufficient. They looked for deeper cuts in charges made to them on the basis that it cost the broker no more to handle their large orders than to handle small ones, and therefore the commission increase should not be in direct ratio to the amount of money and the number of shares involved.

Evidence that the institutions were right in some respects had come to the Street in the form of a practice at once condemned and praised—the give-up (**G**). Assume that an institution would place an order for the purchase of 10,000 shares with a broker. The broker would execute the order. But then he would be directed by the institution to share the commission with other brokers whom, for one reason or another, the institution wanted to please—perhaps brokers who had been supplying research, or who were rendering other services. In many cases, the broker was directed to give up 50%, 60%, or even as much as 80% of his commission to other brokers.

Institutions often choose to have large blocks handled by a single broker for excellent reasons. If 10 brokers handle 1,000 shares each of a 10,000-share trade, there is more chance of leakage—that is, the specialists and others on the floors of the Exchange, not knowing quite what is going on, might think some kind of bad news was pending about the stock in question. The price would drop; perhaps the last 5,000 shares of the 10,000 would sell at a substantially lower price than the first 5,000. But one order executed by one broker for 10,000 shares might be handled in a single transaction or fed judiciously into the market in a series of smaller transactions, while the effects are being carefully watched.

Yet no institution could afford to do business with just one broker all of the time. Everyone has varying needs that involve the various abilities of many brokers—as I have mentioned, research, good execution, favors in former times, and a host of other factors enter in. Accordingly, the practice of give-ups was rooted in the realities of the market.* But so widespread did the practice become, and so nefarious were some of its overtones, that the New York Stock Exchange after a prolonged argument finally had to rule against the give-up. It did so on November 21, 1968.

With institutions no longer able to use the give-up to their own advantage, they bore down hard for another kind of saving—a direct rate decrease. But while they were pressing for lower charges, the institutional houses—that is, the firms that concentrate on large block orders and handle the business of these big financial organizations—were reacting quite the other way. Usually interested only in orders of 5,000 shares or more and having a total lack of interest in the small investor, these institutional houses naturally looked to the upper end of

---

* While the give-up has been largely and properly decried as a business practice, it was not without its good side. It came about, after all, because commission rates were fixed. Had rates been competitive instead of fixed, there would have been no give-up in the first place. Paul Samuelson, the Nobel Prize-winning economist, has said that "competition breathes asthmatically through the give-up."

the commission scale for their bread and butter. So, like such big retail firms as Merrill Lynch, the institutional house had a big stake in the NERA outcome.

To understand the true nature of the conflict here, one must come to grips with some fairly technical explanations. Most of the institutional houses do what is known as "block positioning" (**G**). That is, they actually buy the stock from the selling institutions, own it themselves—briefly, they hope— and then sell it to another institution as quickly as possible. This modus operandi actually constituted a new kind of marketplace arising to some extent from the limitations and inadequacies of the central market. But to the institutions, the block positioners offered a highly desirable outlet. The institution by using block positions is often able to get out of a stock in one swoop at a single price and does not have to worry too much about the effect on the market. (Right now there is a debate over whether institutions owning large blocks of stock are entitled to "instant liquidity.") By dealing with a block positioning house an institution also avoids publicity—so that few people would know, for example, that a large life insurance company had decided to get out of 100,000 shares of a blue-chip stock. Often an institution prefers to trade in that quiet way.

For the block houses, positioning offered good profit—but also the prospect of heavy loss if the market should take a sudden tumble. In a bear market, block positioning loses a good deal of its glow.

As a result, immediately after the NERA proposals were introduced, virtually all parties concerned were at odds. The little man was saying, "Don't raise your prices so high." The institutional brokerage firms were saying, "We can't afford any further cut." And Merrill Lynch, the largest and most influential house, was carving out a position different from both of those.

So the New York Stock Exchange, through its Costs and Revenues Committee (**G**) specializing in this area, was trying to represent a constituency whose interests were conflicting. Further, because of their preoccupation with failing and near-failing firms, the principal officers of the New York Stock Exchange had not taken adequate time to prepare their positions in a political sense—that is, they had not been able to do enough exploring and lobbying among member firms to anticipate and head off public dispute. It is by no means clear that preparation would have spelled success. But lack of it surely spelled defeat.

Meanwhile, the Exchange was caught in other potential conflicts as well. On the one hand, it did not wish to make too much known about the details of the precarious financial condition of its member firms, for fear of a loss of public confidence—which was beginning to drain away anyway. On the other hand, the Exchange had to justify to the SEC an increase in the commission schedule; the most obvious argument to use was the spreading evidence of acute need. The path was a narrow and difficult one. Not everyone who trod it managed to conduct himself as a paragon of wisdom might have done.

As the evidence accumulated that walls on Wall Street were crumbling, the SEC took up a more and more adversary posture. As I've said, it missed a fine chance for an affirmative contribution to the industry that it regulates—and that is also charged with regulating itself. Instead, the SEC grew increasingly angry and hostile because it believed that the Exchange was withholding critically important information about the financial health of member firms.

But the then Chairman of the Exchange, Bernard Lasker, and the President, Robert Haack, were convinced that they could arrange mergers, arrange loans, and otherwise improvise to keep an avalanche from covering the pavements of the Street. On the whole, my judgment is that they managed to do this quite well and quite wisely, although I did not at the time, nor do I at present, find myself in complete agreement with every particular of the means adopted. In the case of Hayden, Stone, to which the Exchange made the loan I described earlier, the behind-the-scenes work turned out to be effective. Finally, a merger was arranged between Hayden, Stone and Walston & Company, and later the merger reached out to include Cogan, Berlin, Weill & Levitt. Without the work of the Exchange's leaders, including Felix Rohatyn of Lazard Frères and Solomon Litt of Asiel & Co., it seems possible that a failure or two, rather than successful mergers, would have taken place. Even with the Stock Exchange's insurance fund, a substantial number of individual customers might have been hurt.

In a sense, too, larger issues were at stake. The "domino theory" cannot be ignored. If a longer chain of failures had in fact taken place, the equivalent of a run on the bank might have materialized. In Wall Street terms, this would mean a wave of demands from customers both to withdraw their securities from the custody of their firms and to withdraw cash balances from their accounts. Assuming that the firms involved had been conducting their business legally—that is, had been segregating securities as required—all of the demands from besieging customers could be met. But to meet them would take time. And in that atmosphere panic might have spread as delays went on. So one must give some credence to the argument advanced by the leaders of the Exchange that everyone's interests, not just the interests of the threatened firms, were best served by avoiding a succession of bankruptcies.

Some SEC actions at the time I find harder to understand. The primary mission of the SEC is not to protect member firms, but to protect the public. It had every right to issue subpoenas if necessary to get details about the financial condition of any member of the industry that it has the responsibility of overseeing. But instead it displayed a tendency to carp, and to generate hostility toward the New York Stock Exchange. The Exchange for its part was failing to convince the regulators of its earnestness and sincerity. So just at a time when the Exchange and SEC ought to have been working very closely together, the staffs of the two organizations were virtually at war. The SEC's staff began to question whether the Exchange had been regulating its members cautiously, equitably, and with rigorous regard for the proper standards.

There could hardly have been a worse time for such a conflict. And the damage remains today as the industry both seeks and is being pressed to change the old modes and methods.

In the spring of 1970 a good deal of the lowering atmosphere was cleared by an unexpected compromise in the field of commission rates. The NERA proposals were simply too battered to survive. As their inequities and complexities emerged, even some of their proponents had to concede that they were inadequate to the demands of the day. At the same time, the evidence that help was needed by brokerage houses was everywhere, even though not always in sufficient detail to satisfy the SEC. The compromise took the form of a "service charge"—one that brought with it no increased service, but did provide an increase in price of $15 or of 50%, whichever was less, on every transaction of 1,000 shares or less.

The amount of $15 was reached in a strictly ad hoc fashion. A small committee run by Salim Lewis, the senior partner of

Bear, Stearns, had spent a good deal of time discussing ways out of the dilemma posed by NERA. I was a member of the Lewis Committee.

Gradually, the conversations of the committee began to swing away from the thought of any permanent change in the commission structure, which was looking more and more impossible to achieve. Attention moved toward an interim, temporary revenue increase that would still bring quick help to the many firms in serious financial trouble. We knew that any alteration in the structure formally labeled "an increase" would appear too permanent, and thus too important, to win the SEC's quick consent. We decided that such consent, to be won, had to be temporary. It is hard to determine exactly at what point in the Lewis Committee discussions who came up with the idea of a surcharge of $15. I recall that at certain points in the discussions I suggested a $10 service charge—which was seriously considered, but finally discarded because some of those present believed it would not result in enough help quickly enough to the firms that were foundering. So the $15 service charge or 50% of the commission charge—whichever is less—was born.

There was no guarantee that the $15 service charge would bail everybody out. Indeed, the initial objective of the proposed change in rates by the New York Stock Exchange was to raise about $450-million in added revenues for the industry at large. But the estimate of the revenues from the service charge, largely because of the stipulation that they could not exceed a maximum of 50%, fell about $150-million short of that desired objective. But even that more modest amount was as attractive to the industry as roast beef to a hungry man.

For its part, the SEC was willing and able to accept such an interim proposal. The increase was subject to easy change or elimination, so that the SEC could not be pilloried for favoring the industry excessively; and the stipulation of a 50% maximum increase stood as evidence of the SEC's interest in the individual investor.

Thus the service charge came into effect in the second week of April 1970.

It had an immediate, stimulating effect. Its imposition was presently followed by the fortuitous but very happy circumstance of improved volume in May, which increased everyone's gross revenues by a greater sum somewhat more quickly than had been anticipated. Quite suddenly, everyone felt better. And the worse their condition, the better they felt. When water is pouring into the hold of a ship, nothing is quite so reassuring as the sound of the bilge pumps.

But, as it turned out, the added revenues from the service charge were only the first of many changes to take place on the Street.

CHAPTER VII

Capital and Its Punishment

THE DETERMINANT OF THE FINANCIAL HEALTH of every firm on the Street is its capital position. A great paradox about Wall Street is that although its experts are the best in the world when it comes to analyzing the capital structure of the corporations they are looking at, and although its sermons to the outside world never fail to include some homilies about the conservative management of capital, the Street in general has managed its own capital poorly. For a long time it was improvident as regards its future and, without fully realizing it, it took up some anti-capitalistic postures.

It seems to me a travesty that Wall Street does not better practice what it preaches. Managers on the Street tell every industry in the country or in the world how it should be capitalized. In their role as investment bankers, Wall Street firms undertake to advise other companies on proper capitalization, on how to determine when new capital is needed, and on how and when to raise it. Yet until 1970 no firm on the Street had raised its own capital by a public issue. During 1970, two firms that were members of the New York Stock Exchange became public companies. The first was Donaldson, Lufkin & Jenrette, a small specialized institutional house that had to precipitate a brisk battle with the New York Stock Exchange in order to go public. The other, far less well known, was Institutional Equity Corp., which operates a small general securities business, including underwriting, in Houston, Texas. In 1971 Merrill Lynch, which had favored public ownership for 10 years or more, made financial history by becoming the first big retail house to go public. Other firms doing a public business have followed.

123

Historically, Wall Street's retrograde position is easy to explain. When the Exchange first started on Wall Street, under the buttonwood tree in 1792, its members were all individuals. They ran their own little firms, taking in money from their brokerage. Whatever profits there were went to them as individual entrepreneurs. Gradually, as the business grew, individuals took in partners. The partnership form of management—general and limited—dominated the Street until as recently as 1953. All during those big years in the 1920s, every firm on the Street was a partnership—there were no corporations. During the 1940s, following World War II, some movement started toward permitting the corporate form, but not until the late '40s and early '50s did the Board of Governors of the New York Stock Exchange take these proposals seriously. Even then, vigorous arguments were launched against incorporation of firms. The arguments, reread today, sound antediluvian. If one looks on 1970 as the Year of the Flood, there is some special meaning to that thought.

Under the partnership mode, every partner in the firm had to sign each year new articles of agreement. When a partner left the firm, he took his capital with him. Were a partner to die, his money would generally have to be withdrawn, although his widow or those running his estate sometimes had the option of keeping a reduced portion at work in the firm in some special form. The names of firms on the Street were those of the senior partners in the firm—which is why the names kept changing so much and why every organization on the Street always seemed to have stationery being engraved at the printers. To this day, I still get asked, "Whatever happened to Beane?"

I can recall myself the day when Merrill Lynch had 117 partners. That made for a huge and unwieldy kind of organization. Theoretically, each partner shared in all of the vicissitudes of a partnership. Each year, new agreements were drawn up, pored over, and then signed by each of the 117 individuals. Whenever there was need for additional capital the managing partner—in our case either Charles E. Merrill, during his long tenure, or Winthrop Smith—would go around to each of the other partners, and ask for additional capital contributions in order to finance Merrill Lynch's growing business.

If the individuals for whatever reason did not choose to put in more capital, then the firm as a whole would elect to take in more partners to raise more money. Everyone coming in as a general partner had to weigh very carefully the responsibilities of general partnerships—he was, quite literally, putting every cent he had at stake. While a limited type of partnership was available, this type was carefully regulated by the New York Stock Exchange, and not over 40% of a firm's capital could be kept in this limited form.

One great danger from the partnership form comes when such firms, rather than incorporating and putting stock in the hands of their employees, or becoming public corporations as they now may, choose instead to go to outside sources. Given the old environment of the Street, where everybody knew everybody and so much depended on whom you knew, the most likely outside source would be a wealthy client. Under those circumstances, the head of the firm or another general partner would go to that wealthy client and propose to him that he make an investment in the firm. A common form of such an investment came to be what is known as a "subordinated account"—a hazardous and to my mind thoroughly undesirable way of raising capital, and a device that can be held responsible for a great many of the agonies inflicted on the Street in 1970.

The device worked as follows. Assume that a customer of a New York Stock Exchange firm had $200,000 in securities in his account with that firm. The general partner asked him if he would care to subordinate his right to those securities to the claims of other customers and creditors. The customer in return for so doing earned perhaps an additional 4% or so on the value of his investment, while to all intents and purposes this money continued to be managed as it was before. In other words, he stood to gain in this example another $8,000 a year, with no particular added effort and what at one time anyway was only minimal risk. As for the borrowing firm, it could now report to the New York Stock Exchange that it had an additional $200,000 of capital, less a certain reduction.

But the experience of 1970 lighted up the hazards. The securities in this example are worth $200,000 on this particular day. But they are of course subject to market fluctuation. Tomorrow they might be worth $250,000, thus adding still more to the capital of the member firm and allowing it to borrow against that capital an added sum. But securities have an unfortunate way of falling in value sometimes. In a period of market decline, perhaps the portfolio of the customer we are speaking of might drop to $150,000 or even $100,000. The market decline usually corresponds with periods of low volume and low profits for brokerage houses, including as an illustration the period of which we are now speaking. So the client would find himself looking at double trouble—shrinking value in his portfolio, and a commitment to a securities firm that suddenly appeared far less solid and substantial than he formerly assumed it to be.

Clients, good or bad, are also human beings. And, under the circumstances which I am describing, the client is sure to respond as a human being would. In short, he wants out. Usually, he will have agreed when he made his subordinated loan to leave it in the firm only for a limited period of time— 12 months being a common length. So now he starts counting off the weeks, and the instant it becomes legally possible for him to withdraw his capital from the firm he does so. A firm heavily capitalized by subordinated loans is thus exposed to a good deal of risk. It has impermanent capital subject to market fluctuations—two characteristics that can combine to produce disastrous results.

Of course the general partners in the hypothetical firm I am describing could always flesh out its capital position by putting in more money themselves. But the chances are good that their assets have limits. Furthermore, they may be heavily invested, themselves in stocks, whose value at this moment in time has declined. They are unlikely to want to sell securities at a loss in order to put cash into their firm—a much more likely expedient would be simply to pledge the securities as capital. In brief, they would probably put up stock—which like the stock of the subordinated lender I have just described, and all other kinds as well, is subject to fluctuation.

New rules of the New York Stock Exchange, passed in 1971 —after the horrendous experiences of the previous year—have corrected some of these dangers. Borrowing ratios have been changed. The length of time for which subordinated loans can be made has been extended, and there are circumstances under which they cannot be withdrawn—especially when withdrawal would weaken the firm. All that has resulted in a substantial improvement. But we had to go through 1970 first.

A less crucial but still bewildering outgrowth of the partnership form is the number of name changes, and the consequent loss of public identity that it entails. After a merger in 1940, Merrill Lynch was called Merrill Lynch, E. A. Pierce & Cassatt. Within a year, a very well known brokerage house by the name of Fenner & Beane, which was born as a cotton house in the south and extended its business in securities to the north, joined Merrill Lynch, E. A. Pierce & Cassatt. Then the Cassatt name was dropped. The firm became Merrill Lynch, Pierce, Fenner & Beane.

Merrill Lynch, of course, was actually two people. Charles E. Merrill and Edmund C. Lynch met before World War I, struck up a friendship and decided to start a Wall Street house. Charles Merrill himself told me that the first stationery they ordered came back from the printers bearing the legend "Merrill Lynch & Co." Since they had spent what was then to them quite a lot of money on the printing, they were not of a mind to pay for the stationery a second time merely for the sake of a comma between Merrill and Lynch. They decided they could not afford a comma—or at least not right away. By the time the need for a second stationery order rolled around, the firm was already a success. Merrill and Lynch decided not to change the original name. No comma has ever come between Merrill and Lynch, and publicity worth countless millions has resulted—to be added, of course, to the initial saving at the printer.

A later episode in Merrill Lynch's history illustrates another difficulty with the partnership form of organization. Charles Merrill died in 1956. Winthrop Smith became both managing partner and directing partner—the equivalent in corporate terms of both chairman of the board and president. In 1957 Smith decided that the time had come to choose a second man—again, in corporate terms, the equivalent of appointing a president. His selection was Michael W. McCarthy, a choice that Smith announced at a partners' meeting on a Monday in October 1957. I can vouch for the fact that the selection of McCarthy was generally approved—except for one lone and loud dissenting voice.

The voice came from Alpheus C. Beane, a son of one of the founders of Fenner & Beane, and a strong-minded man. Alph Beane could think of no better candidate for the job than himself. He made no bones about expressing his view before the other partners. After Smith made his announcement, Beane promptly stood up and spelled out in detail the reasons for his disappointment. He recounted his own credentials. The other partners, of whom I was one, listened to Alph, but did not agree with him. In the following vote, McCarthy's selection was endorsed.

After the general meeting, Alph Beane met with a small subcommittee of the board of partners. Alph was told that if he could not wholeheartedly accept the decision of the general partners, then perhaps it would be better for him to leave the

firm. Still in high dudgeon, Alph agreed that he would leave—
and besides taking his money, he also would take his name
along with him. Merrill Lynch, in short, could no longer end
with a Beane. The partners decided that if that was what Alph
wanted, that is what Alph would get. In place of Beane, the
partners voted the name of Smith, in honor of the then-
principal member of the firm.

While Merrill Lynch was already a firm of celebrity, the
change of the final name from Beane to Smith attracted a
great deal more attention. Journalists explained it; editorial
writers decried it; and there was a general public comment
taking the form of "Merrill Lynch, Pierce, Fenner *and Smith,
yet?*"

With the change of name, of course, all stationery, calling
cards, forms, and all manner of legal documents had to be
changed correspondingly. The costs to Merrill Lynch for printing bills, as I recall, was in the neighborhood of $100,000. But
I think we got 10 times that amount in publicity. As for Alph
Beane, he soon resumed his friendship with his former partners. After he left Merrill Lynch, he moved to another brokerage house, which became known as J. R. Williston & Beane.
During the Ira Haupt salad oil scandal, whose outlines have
already been sketched, Merrill Lynch lent Williston & Beane
enough money to tide it over a difficult period. Today, Alph
Beane is an officer of Reynolds Securities Inc., a well-known
and prosperous member of the New York Stock Exchange.

This Beane-sized experience, while insignificant in itself,
pointed up some of the absurdities of the partnership form of
management. With some other forward-looking houses, Merrill Lynch had already taken the lead in trying to persuade
the New York Stock Exchange to change its policy against
incorporation. The chief argument against incorporation—
namely that the brokerage business, like the business of a
lawyer or an accountant or a doctor, depends on personal
relationships—was really obsolete. Banks have trust departments; doctors work in groups and now even incorporate; and
personal relationships are not barred by the corporate form
of management. Those arguing in favor of incorporation took
the view that people would be more comfortable dealing
with firms that took a more permanent form, rather than
leading the day-to-day existence of a partnership. After all,
in many Wall Street partnerships one man has a controlling
financial interest—perhaps as much as 75% or 80% of the

capital. I pointed out often that were he to move on to other pastures, his firm would be placed in the very awkward position of having to replace his capital within a few months or go out of business. A corporation, which would have a sounder capital structure, would result in a stronger, rather than a weaker, relationship with customers.

Finally in 1953 the notion that firms might metamorphose into corporations was accepted as permissible by the New York Stock Exchange. By the end of 1970 a total of 572 organizations formed the New York Exchange. Of that number, 353 were partnerships and 219 were corporations. Most of the partnerships are the specialist firms working on the floor of the Exchange, while the majority of the firms that do a public business, especially the larger of these, are incorporated. Until 1971, F. I. du Pont, Glore Forgan & Co. was a great exception. It remained a partnership until Ross Perot became its principal equity holder. Two other big houses doing business with the public, Paine Webber Jackson & Curtis and Reynolds Securities, remained partnerships until they became publicly owned corporations.

In 1959 Merrill Lynch completed the long and tedious process of conversion and became a corporation. We have never regretted the change, especially in view of our longer-range goal of going public.

Doubtless to assume the corporate form was to take a progressive step. But the corporate form does not bring with it automatically the single most desirable feature of any company: the permanence of its capital. Twenty people may form a corporation and each put up $100,000, thus forming a company worth $2-million in capital. But if one of the founders dies, the corporation has to pay out of its own treasury an amount equal to what he invested. That leaves the corporation, obviously, with the need to find some means of replacing the withdrawn amount. Private corporations have some of the disadvantages of partnerships.

So while the process of incorporation carried with it a solution to part of the Street's capital difficulties, it by no means solved them all. The more significant step was clearly the next one—becoming a public corporation. That means, pursuing the example I have just given, that at some point in time the founders of the corporation put on sale to the public an amount of stock equal to the capital that is needed or wanted at the time. The creation of a public market obviates the possibility of a sudden withdrawal of a significant amount of capital from the corporation, and the consequent danger.

Whether the value of the stock after issue goes up or down is not the point. The point is that there is created a two-way market, some people wanting to buy and some wanting to sell. All of these transactions take place away from the site of the original corporation. The corporation may still have, to some degree, its fate and future tied up with the value of the stock, but it is free from concern about a sudden, unforeseen capital withdrawal that could hurt or kill it. All corporations with stock listed on the New York Stock Exchange are of course in this situation. Indeed, this constitutes the essence of the New York Stock Exchange's raison d'être.

But at this juncture it was difficult for Wall Street to achieve such a metamorphosis. Although the Stock Exchange in principle favored public ownership for others, particularly for corporations large enough to be listed on the Exchange, it did not apply the same principles to brokerage firms. Once again it could not bring itself to practice what it preached.

Merrill Lynch had barely got through the process of incorporation before it began to push for public ownership. In 1961 Michael McCarthy, then chairman of the board, pointed out all of the compelling reasons for public ownership to Keith Funston, who was President of the New York Exchange at the time. Neither the officials of the Exchange nor its members greeted the idea with much enthusiasm. They felt that Merrill Lynch was simply serving its own interest in advancing the proposal. Once it had become a public corporation, Merrill Lynch would be able to squeeze everybody else out of business, and the Exchange would be hurt. That argument was as old as capitalism: it has been applied to supermarket chains, to retail stores, and to a thousand other enterprises. Merrill Lynch had to persist for three years before the Exchange would even admit that the proposal merited the formation of a committee to investigate and report on its feasibility.

Avery Patrick Rockefeller Jr., then a partner of Dominick & Dominick, became chairman of the committee. I served as a member of it for its entire six-year life. Except for the Costs and Revenue Committee, which as we have seen deals with the vital matter of commissions, this public ownership committee probably was the longest-lived of any ever formed by the Exchange. Meeting after meeting was held, argument after argument advanced, and the years ticked by—but nothing happened. During the period of great growth on the Street, in 1967 and 1968, when the present and future needs for permanent capital became so apparent to many, the committee languished.

Finally, in 1968, it had to abandon its passivity. Stunned by the growth in volume and the obvious dangers of volatile capital, the committee—in an act that under the circumstances was hardly dramatic—went so far as to recommend that the New York Stock Exchange permit public ownership of the debentures (**G**) of member firms. In that way, instead of issuing common stock, the firm could borrow money from the public, pay the going rate of interest, and later pay off its debt. This would permit the firm's members to raise the capital they needed and in fact were pressing for the right to raise, but would not give any ownership to the public. The debenture holder, of course, would share in neither profits nor losses, but merely collect interest on the amount he had lent out. He would get no voice in management.

The difficulty with the issuance of debentures by member firms arose from one of those great exterior forces that played such havoc with every phase of financial life at this time. Climbing interest rates enabled lenders to ask and get 7 1/2% for their money in the early part of 1969 and as much as 8 1/2% later on in the year. Wall Street firms were not by and large looked on as prime investments—indeed, some of them were clearly the worst of risks, rather than the best. A reasonable expectation, therefore, was that member organizations would have to pay in the neighborhood of 9% or even as much as 10% to debenture holders. My judgment is that there was a moment in early 1970 when debentures of brokerage houses would have been hard to sell at 11% or 12%. Such rates would seem to preclude the wisdom of borrowing. Consequently, I know of no member firm that ever sold debentures to the general public. A good many firms sold debentures to various institutions privately over the years, but I don't believe that any did so at this critical juncture.

The small, specialized and aggressive firm of Donaldson, Lufkin & Jenrette became the first to become publicly owned. With surprising force and speed, it pushed through its intention to go public. Although a partner in the firm was a member of the Board of Governors of the Exchange, the firm told the Board flatly that the Exchange was following a wrong course in forbidding member firms to go public, and—to the shock and horror of many members of the investment community—announced publicly that Donaldson, Lufkin would file a registration statement immediately with the SEC as a preliminary to becoming a public corporation. Although Merrill Lynch had been the first to declare in principle for public ownership, our firm did not muscle the proposal through— partly, I believe, because of the reaction entailed in such a move by the largest and strongest firm in the industry.

Donaldson, Lufkin's action had immediate consequences on both the Board of Governors of the New York Stock Exchange and the SEC. Outspoken on many issues, SEC had generally kept its peace on the subject of going public. While in the past I had heard staff members argue against the principle, no formal position was taken either by the former Chairman of the SEC, Manny Cohen—who was so candid in many other areas—or by other commissioners until this moment, when the issue could no longer be avoided. I believe many members of the Board of Governors of the Exchange had also been simply hoping that the whole question would go away.

Now, however, no further equivocation was possible. Either the Exchange had to excommunicate Donaldson, Lufkin, or it had to accommodate that firm as a public corporation.

The course of accommodation was chosen. Guided by Pat Rockefeller, the Public Ownership Committee adopted appropriate proposals, including those that had long been suggested by Merrill Lynch. One of the new rules stated that any new issue had to be made for the purpose of raising capital. Certain other provisions that also sought to safeguard the public from being mulcted were pushed through. Finally, both the New York Stock Exchange and the SEC gave their approval to this fundamental change in the nature and character of the Street.

Donaldson, Lufkin went public on April 9, 1970. That was some months after the filing of the original prospectus. Between the two periods (as we have seen) great events had taken place—few of them encouraging for those who might be considering an investment in a securities firm. So when Donaldson's stock finally went on sale over-the-counter, the issue price was considerably below that predicted only a few months before. The stock was issued at $15 per share, a multiple of 14.3 times its annual earnings the year before. The subsequent action of the stock also proved disappointing. It has fluctuated between a low of 5 in June 1970, and a high

of 18 7/8 in April 1971. On September 1, 1971, a year and
a half after its issue date, it was selling at 11 1/8. That represented a high rebound from the low of $5 a share in June
1970, but still stood below the issue price. Like most other
firms on the Street, Donaldson, Lufkin had sharply reduced
earnings for the first six months of 1970. But for the first nine
months of 1971, the firm had revenues of over $25-million,
and an after-tax net of over $5-million.

The true significance of going public, however, does not lie
with the modest or outstanding success of any particular issue
of equity in a Wall Street firm. The radical change comes with
the permanent nature of the capital once a firm is owned by
the public.

In difficult moments on Wall Street, there is always a danger
that the hand of self-regulation will relax its grip. We have
already reviewed the reasons why the New York Stock Exchange, as the principal self-regulatory body concerned, was
not inclined in 1968, 1969 and 1970 to look too closely at
the nature of the securities that sponsors of the firm were
pledging as capital. The Exchange tended to accept the statement of the member firm and its auditors (who incidentally
are now coming under fire for the role they played—or perhaps it is more precise to say the role they failed to play—in
this trying time) that the stock had been pledged as capital,
that it had a certain value, and that its proceeds were being
used generally in the firm's business.

The consequences of such an attitude—which I in my personal judgment must call lax—were starkly illustrated in the
case of Gregory & Sons. The authorities of the New York
Stock Exchange were rudely surprised when Gregory & Sons
came to them with the unexpected point-blank announcement
that the firm was about to go into bankruptcy. The Exchange
had no idea that Gregory's condition was so precarious. The
basic flaw turned out to be that Gregory's capital was illiquid
—that not only had the firm come to rely heavily for its capital
on securities pledged by its partners, which was undesirable
enough, but also that the securities themselves took the particularly unattractive and largely unnegotiable form of letter
stock.

Now assume, if you will, that a member firm of the New
York Stock Exchange needs capital to buy stock in the open
market in order to replace box or dividend differences. If a
large part of its capital is made up of letter stock, it has very

little room for maneuver. It cannot sell the letter stock to raise cash because to do so would be illegal.* And if its other forms of capital are already supporting debt or otherwise committed, the firm, regardless of the season, finds itself on thin ice.

To revert to the case of Gregory & Sons, bankruptcy did overtake the firm. Immediately afterward, the New York Stock Exchange had to draw on the special trust fund set up by the Exchange and contributed by its members to ensure that none of Gregory's customers would suffer losses of either securities or cash. All the members of the Exchange were forced to make a contribution from their income because one of its members took a position in the market that could not be easily liquidated and that was known to be precarious in the first place. I have never been able fully to understand why there was no outcry against the practice of acceptance of letter stock immediately following this regrettable affair. It took some time before amendments to Rule 325 governing letter stock was worked out—indeed, it took too long.

That so much time was required, points up the unhappy propensity of the members of the Exchange community to move from crisis to crisis without seeking to address themselves to the underlying causes of any of them. To that must be added a kind of "let the devil take the hindmost" expediency that may serve the ephemeral interest of a few fly-by-night operators, but works against the long-range interest of the people who are serious about the business and intend to remain in it. Such attitudes must change if the Stock Exchange is going to have a future (which Bob Haack, now retiring as the Exchange's president, seems as his term ends to doubt).

Since the time of Gregory & Sons, there is plenty of evidence that the attitudes are changing, although more out of compulsion than choice. The road which the Exchange was now forced to take was clearly marked with some pretty obvious signs—but too few people had chosen to read them.

To be fair about all this, I should add that I see no objection whatever to member firms investing in the market or speculating in other ways with their own capital if they want

* Until January 1972, the SEC had never ruled on how long letter stock must be held before it can be sold. This particular point illustrates a more general deficiency, about which I have long argued with the Commission and its staff. The deficiency is one that in my less cheerful moments I am inclined to attribute to the legal profession at large: namely, the practice of making rules by decision in particular cases and leaving the ruling open to all kinds of future interpretations, instead of ruling for present and future as well.

to. But their capital position should be sufficient to support their aggregate indebtedness, and to service and protect their customers, before those other practices are condoned. If member firms regard speculation as a way to profit, then let them speculate; but let them provide for the essentials of their business, and let them give a thought to the general reputation and position of the entire financial community, before they do so. Firms doing business with the public should be allowed to speculate in securities, commodities or whatever other investment risks they select only with their excess capital— not with the capital that supports aggregate indebtedness and their public reputation.

In all businesses assets can be leveraged. In Wall Street the leverage has particular significance. Under the rules of the New York Stock Exchange, a member firm must regularly add up all of its liabilities and compare them with its capital. The sum of the liabilities of the organization—that is, the money owed by the firm to its customers, to other brokers, to banks and to anyone else—are all debts of the member firm. Until mid-1971, that aggregate indebtedness could not exceed 20 times the firm's net capital. But if any member firm got to the point where its liabilities exceeded its capital by a 15-to-1 ratio, then, in theory at least, warnings were sounded, and the New York Stock Exchange would step in to question the firm about its activities. What it now proposed to do was to bring its ratio down below 15-to-1.

For some time, Merrill Lynch argued in public and in the Exchange's private councils that the 20-to-1 ratio was too high—and that no member firm's liabilities should be permitted to exceed its capital by more than a multiple of 10 or 12. We believed this would be a much safer ratio. We also suggested that the warning signs should be given at a comparably earlier period. Partly because of our urging, the whole subject underwent lengthy and complicated debate by a committee of the New York Stock Exchange for several years— the complications involving such matters as "haircutting" (**G**).

Much sounder capital rules resulted. The ratio was lowered. Warnings go off sooner. And the rules governing subordinated loans have been made much more stringent, leaving the firm far safer—if the value of the securities should fall or the leader want to withdraw—than the former practices did.

But at the time of the Gregory & Sons debacle, in May 1970, the old rules were still in effect. And, although the fact is not apparent at first glance, they permitted a kind of triple layer of borrowing. If, to postulate a case, one of the partners of a firm needed but did not have $100,000 to put up as capital and establish himself as a general partner, he could go to a bank and borrow the money. Or perhaps, in a convoluted deal not without its comic overtones, the firm itself might lend him the money. In either case, the $100,000 is not really cash capital, but only a loan. Against that loan, the firm can pile on loans of its own. So the stated capital, against which aggregate indebtedness is heaped, would be neither so large nor so strong as it appeared. That makes a jerry-built structure, to which all kinds of Gothic additions can be tacked on.

And many of the very firms that conducted business under such leaky roofs were advising publicly held corporations about the best way for those corporations to raise money, and telling them how to build a solid foundation of capital on which to grow and expand.

So, to sum up the conditions in which most firms found themselves, their capital was being eaten into by box differences and dividend differences, caused by the paper crunch that accompanied the heavy volume of the immediately preceding years. At the same time, in a sense the capital being consumed was not really there at all—or at least not there in the form in which it was commonly understood to be there. A firm that had $2-million in capital invested in common stocks suddenly found itself with only $1-million, and had to reduce its aggregate indebtedness from, let us say, $30-million to $15-million—a process requiring some pretty radical pruning.

Hayden, Stone and Dempsey-Tegeler were by no means the only firms caught in this twin-jawed trap. Many members of the Board of Governors of the New York Stock Exchange, greatly worried by the condition in which they found the member organizations, had stacked on top of that worry a more personal worry of their own—the condition of the firm to which they belonged.

It was all very alarming. With its eye on the public investor, the Congress took cognizance of the situation, and decided it was time to act.

The beginnings of congressional interest became apparent as early as 1969, when Senator Edmund Muskie of Maine introduced an insurance bill in the Senate. The bill had the general purpose of protecting the individual investor should his broker fail. At the time, little attention—much too little, as later events were to reveal—was given to the Muskie bill. The New York Stock Exchange had then some $25-million, consisting of $15-million in cash and $10-million in credits, set aside in its special trust fund for insurance of customers against a broker's failure. Few principals on the Street could believe that such a sum would not be adequate to cover any present or prospective failures. But their confidence in that fact, at first privately and then publicly, soon began to diminish in the face of hard reality. That decline of confidence was matched by a corresponding upsurge of interest in the Muskie bill.

Senator Muskie's concern did not spring from any special desire to win more votes in his home state. Both in absolute numbers and in terms of percentages, the State of Maine does not have a great many individual shareholders. The New York Stock Exchange census taken in 1970 shows that Maine had at that time only 214,000 stockholders out of a total population of 20-million. To put this in perspective, Rhode Island had 122,000, Iowa had 202,000, Kansas 221,000 shareholders. The big, populous states of course had many more: New Jersey had over a million, and Pennsylvania nearly a million and a half. Nonetheless, seeing a chance for leadership, Senator Muskie was the first to call for government protection for investors.

Over the course of more than a year his bill went through many forms. As finally passed before congressional adjournment in December 1970, it provided the individual shareholder with a kind of protection against the failure of his brokerage house roughly analogous to the protection that the Federal Deposit Insurance Corporation, set up in 1933, affords depositors in the event of bank failures.

Wall Street has a bad habit of recognizing and responding to public opinion and public needs only when the time is already very late. In this case, only after talk of hearings in connection with the Muskie bill began to spread, the state of public opinion became glaringly obvious, and the seriousness of congressional intent became evident, did the industry start to develop its own proposals. Then at last a committee was formed by the New York Stock Exchange under the chairmanship of Gus Levy, senior partner of Goldman Sachs, to consider alternatives to Government action. The key finding of the committee, on which I served, was made early on—the admission among its members that the $25-million in the New

York Stock Exchange trust fund was inadequate to the present day and the prevailing circumstances. There was of course no mathematical way to determine what would constitute an ample fund, but, in part no doubt because of a general affection for round figures, the members of the committee decided that the sum of $100-million would both in fact and in the public view be considered sufficient.

The committee members took full cognizance of the urgency of the matter. Enlargement of the Stock Exchange's fund could await neither legislative action nor a long and complicated trip through the New York Stock Exchange's rule-making mechanisms. As a tribune of urgency, the committee—following a suggestion that first came from Cliff Michel, then of Loeb, Rhoades—decided on a quicker course. It proposed that the fund could be more than doubled by simply transferring to the fund money that had been set aside to erect a new building to house the New York Stock Exchange. The Exchange's plans were to build a large structure at the foot of Wall Street on the East River, where old piers were to be torn down, fill brought in, and offices and a new trading floor put up.

As it turned out, to put up a new building while old ones, symbolically at least, were on the verge of collapse, was impossible. After as close a look as they could get at the conditions of various member firms of the Exchange, the committee promptly recommended to the Board of Governors that a different and better use be made of the $30-million already raised for the new building. Technically, what the Board did was vote to earmark temporarily the special building fund of $30-million as part of the trust fund, thus making it available for the protection of customers of member firms threatened by failure. In effect, this action amounted to the transfer of the $30-million to the insurance fund. Indeed, in the end that entire sum was paid out for insurance purposes. The new building became, and remains, a mirage. Discussing in public the future of the New York Stock Exchange, I commented that "One thing about the Exchange's future seems certain: it will be located at the corner of Broad and Wall."

The transfer gave the fund a total of $45-million in cash, in addition to its standby commitment of $10-million by some major New York banks. An effort was made by the President of the New York Exchange to enlarge that standby commitment to a range of $55- to $65-million, and some preliminary meetings with the New York banks, as well as with a few from outside the area, indicated that this might be an achievable goal. But the attempt disappeared amidst the subsequent discussions over the Muskie bill in Congress. Similarly lost were suggestions for putting into the insurance fund all the profits from the New York Stock Exchange, which over the last five years totaled more than $20-million. Since this was my idea, I regarded, and continue to regard, the logic behind it as unassailable: there seems little point in the Stock Exchange accumulating profits and paying taxes on them, while at the same time taxing its members for an insurance fund to protect the public. But time passed that proposal by as well.

Soon it became apparent that no industry plan for insurance was going to materialize that would encompass all the financial, political, and psychological needs. The Street was just too late in recognizing the dimensions of the problem and in fitting its actions to meet those dimensions. Congressional legislation was inevitable.

In sorrowful recognition of the inevitable, the industry changed its strategy. It formed a task force headed by Ralph De Nunzio, a partner of Kidder, Peabody, and then Vice Chairman of the Board of Governors of the New York Stock Exchange. (In 1971 De Nunzio was elected Chairman, succeeding Bernard Lasker.) De Nunzio and his group worked long and tirelessly in an effort to thrash out with the Securities and Exchange Commission a proposal for investor insurance that would satisfy the SEC, the Congress, and the industry itself. That was no easy task. Any delegation from the New York Stock Exchange was bound to be suspected when it appeared in Washington under those circumstances.

In its early versions, the language of the Muskie bill appeared to set up a new layer of regulation over the industry, separate from the SEC and from the self-regulatory bodies, but still possessing great although vague regulatory powers. This prospect was disturbing to many of the industry managers, including myself. I joined in the then-current sentiment that while the industry might need better regulation, it did not need simply more of it, especially coming from a new and untried body of regulators.

At the same time, there was no withstanding the public forces at work. The forces included the Administration in Washington, with even President Nixon himself at one point endorsing the concept of investor insurance. At one time there were floating around a Muskie draft insurance bill, a draft from Wall Street's leaders, and various other indications of general desiderata, some in written form from the SEC and the executive branch. While we were then amidst the flowers in May, the question proved so complex and prolonged that it was not resolved until the snows of December, and then it was resolved in great haste.

The Securities Investor Protection Corporation (SIPC) is the consequence. I serve on its Board of Directors. Its funds, through a tax on the gross revenues of broker-dealers, are gradually building up. They stand now at $35 million, and they should reach $150 million within five years. The legislation bringing SIPC into being is not perfect, but it is workable. Its protection promises to be more than adequate to any foreseeable needs. While it provides a $1-billion line of credit to the U.S. Treasury under certain emergency circumstances, SIPC is unlikely ever to draw on that line of credit. It is not a government agency; if it ever does use its Treasury credits, the Treasury is to be repaid with interest.

Besides their application to the SIPC insurance plan, political overtones colored every event and near-event in that month of May—the fateful month whose narrative began this book. Developments far from the United States—besides Cambodia, whose impact we have already observed—dragged with them a long train of unforeseen or exaggerated consequences. In Europe, financial history was written by Investors Overseas Services, Ltd. IOS was a Geneva-based financial complex running a group of mutual funds, powered by aggressive salesmanship, sold only outside the United States, and, late in history, publicly held. Its funds were large holders of American securities; but still, not much relationship appeared to pertain between IOS, a public corporation, and the health of the economy at home. But as the IOS empire, led by the adventurous Bernie Cornfeld, began to shake apart, those people who held shares in its mutual funds became nervous and began to sell.

Large blocks of stock for sale thus showed up on the New York Stock Exchange. This had a depressing effect on both prices and spirits. Earnings of the IOS parent dropped as well, and the stock went down from a price in the mid-20s to as little as $2 per share. Struggles within IOS found their way garishly into the public press, again with unhappy consequences here at home. Psychologically, the disastrous affair contributed to far-reaching results well beyond the scale of the original event. Indeed, a year or more after the IOS affair it became evident that the conduct and near-collapse of the IOS was part of the process that weakened the United States dollar in relation to European currencies.* From the weakening grew the eventual formal devaluation of the dollar by an increase in the price of gold from $35 to $38 an ounce.

Thus do great events grow from financial sports.

* The story of the IOS empire has already provided meat for several books, the best of which, in my judgment, is called *Do You Sincerely Want To Be Rich?*

CHAPTER VIII

Washington and
Wall Street

WHILE THE REVERBERATIONS FROM *IOS*'S TUR-
moil were being heard, other offshore funds were tottering.
The best known of these was Gramco, which, like IOS, had a
good number of celebrated American personalities associated
with it. And, as the shakiness of offshore funds slowed down
markets and spirits at home, domestic events were taking shape
that would lead to the sensational three days in May.

In regular communication with the Nixon Administration,
Bernard Lasker pressed Wall Street's case during the crisis
that was shaping up. Lasker drove home the significance of
the failures on the Street to the President's official family. He
told various members of that family that only a few people in
Wall Street believed that the President's economic advisers
were on the right track, or that the "game plan," described
earlier, would work. Lasker was urging recognition of the fact
that between Washington and Wall Street lay a special kind of
credibility gap, and, indeed, the gap probably had sprung up
between Washington and the rest of the business community
as well. Out of Lasker's conversations was born the idea, which
I touched on in an earlier chapter, that the President might
host a dinner at the White House to talk intimately with some
Wall Street leaders. Later the idea was expanded to include not
just the Street but other parts of the business world also.

Initially, the news of the dinner was tightly held. The first
public inkling appeared in the *New York Times* on May 23,
when Terry Robards, who covers Wall Street for the *Times*
(and covers it very well), reported that Henry Kissinger and
Budget Director Robert Mayo were soon to meet with a group
of top businessmen, including members of the financial community, to discuss the stock markets and the apparently de-

pressing effect that any and every Government action seemed to have on them.

Robards' report was accurate in every detail. He related that Lasker had had conversations with the President, and then had reported them to the Board of Governors of the New York Stock Exchange. As Robards said, Lasker told the Board that he had passed on to the President an analysis of what was wrong with the market—stressing to the President that the uncertainty about the Vietnam war and the disclosure of a growing Federal budgetary deficit were especially upsetting.

These two topics accounted for the selection of Kissinger and Mayo as spokesmen. Vietnam and the Cambodian invasion clearly fell within Kissinger's area of competence, while the budgetary deficit belonged to Mayo. Robards reported, again correctly, that Lasker had told the President that, besides declining stock prices, businessmen were disturbed by the spreading talk about the possibility of wage and price controls. And Lasker informed President Nixon that his analysis of the various alarming factors at work was based on conversations he had had the previous day with four leaders from the financial community. The conversations were held with Louis Lundborg, then Chairman of the Bank of America; George Champion, retired Chairman of Chase Manhattan; Henry Kaufman, a partner and the chief economist at Salomon Brothers, the largest bond firm and a leading institutional brokerage house; and with me—then the President of Merrill Lynch.

Gradually the plans for the meeting that would bridge the credibility gap began to unfold. Finally, announcement of the dinner was made officially on Tuesday, May 26, and the date was set for the following day—Wednesday, May 27. It seems to me an indication of just how hungry everybody was for good news that the market reacted so favorably to a coming event which, after all, was of itself hardly earth-shaking in importance. Yet the announcement was enough to spark the largest one-day rise in the market's history, as we have seen earlier.

There is always a special aura about dinner at the White House. On this occasion, 63 guests assembled at 8:00 P.M. Of them, 35 came from the Wall Street community: 14 were industrialists; seven were bankers, from various parts of the country; five were heads of big mutual or pension funds; and two came from insurance companies. On hand to greet the guests were some of the leading lights of the Administration.

From the Cabinet came Secretary of the Treasury David Kennedy, Attorney General John Mitchell, and Secretary of Commerce Maurice Stans. Paul McCracken, then Chairman of the President's Council of Economic Advisers, was there, along with Arthur Burns, in his new capacity as Chairman of the Board of Governors of the Federal Reserve. From the President's personal staff came Peter Flanigan, who is charged with liaison between the White House and businessmen and the various Federal agencies that are concerned with business. Among other people present who were close to the President were Charles Colson, special counsel to the President, and William L. Safire, the speech writer who specializes on economic matters. Despite the earlier reports, neither Kissinger nor Mayo was present. Dinner was in the State dining room, at a large square table. Dessert was served promptly on schedule at 9:30 P.M.

After dinner the President rose to talk to his guests. I took careful notes. He started off by saying that he thought the economy would turn up in the third and fourth quarters of the year. He said that the money stock had been increasing just before Dr. Burns took over at the Fed at an annual rate of 5%; but recently, under Burns, the increase had been doubled to 10%. He expressed regret over rising unemployment, warned that it might worsen for a while, and indicated his hope that it would not rise much more.

Then he turned to Cambodia. A huge map of Southeast Asia had been set up behind him, and the President referred to it as he explained the military strategy lying behind the thrust then under way. The President indicated that in his judgment the Cambodian operation should have a bullish effect on the stock market. He explained that the Cambodian move would not run up military expenditures, but in fact might constitute a long-run economy, since it would shorten the war and speed up the return of our troops from Vietnam. He expressed understanding of the fact that the invasion had brought to a boil a good deal of dissension, particularly among young people on the campuses. But he renewed his pledge that he would pull the troops out on time, and stated that this, in turn, would demonstrate to college students that he was keeping his promises, and that the Vietnam war was gradually winding down.

As for the Paris negotiations, the President expressed the view that they might move more quickly as the result of this Cambodian action. He regretted that the invasion had not been widely accepted publicly for what in fact it was: a well thought-out, fast-moving, well-executed and successful coup. He characterized it as the best strike by American forces since General MacArthur landed American forces at Inchon, but admitted that there was no public recognition of the fact. He finished his informal talk by repeating assurances that our troops would be out of Cambodia on schedule, if not ahead of it, and that the withdrawal of American troops from Vietnam would continue as planned.

After the President finished speaking, Lasker rose to explain the Street's perspective. (That, by the way, is often quite different from the perspective of the man in the street.) Lasker said that Wall Street was convinced that certain actions outside of the Street's normal sphere of interest were required before we could expect substantial recovery of the market. One of those actions was close adherence to the schedule of withdrawal announced when the Cambodian strike began. Another, closer to the Street's proper business, was a clear assurance that the Fed would take all the proper steps to support the price of Government bonds. At that time, Government bonds were selling at very heavy discounts—the lowest prices in recent history—with a deterioration of confidence in the bond market in general as a consequence. Finally, Lasker stressed that the Fed should continue to make money more plentiful.

At that point, the President called on Burns to speak to the matter of the money supply. Responding, Burns told the guests that he very well understood and sympathized with their nervousness about the shortage of liquidity. Indeed, he said that the Fed had taken extraordinary steps, following an unusual all-day meeting on the subject, to allay that nervousness. He stressed that the Fed was aware of its responsibilities as a lender of last resort and indicated that it had every intention of properly meeting those responsibilities. Burns declared that the Fed would not be handicapped by any rigid adherence to any theoretical formula affecting the money supply—demonstrating his considerable sensitivity to current practical needs. He also emphasized that, while the Fed would not finance inflation, it had the ability and every intention to meet the country's monetary requirements. I recall vividly my impression that once the current near crisis of liquidity was past, and once the obvious need for some easing in the money supply was behind us, Burns would be very inflation-conscious. His public positions assumed and expressed before the freeze of August 15, 1971, were to bear out this impression.

Following Burns' talk, the President, acting as the leader of a seminar on the economy, asked whether anyone present had any questions. The first came from John Bogle, the head of the Wellington Management Company in Philadelphia. Bogle asked about the young people in the country and how the President was going to deal with their attitudes. The President briefly characterized the mood of young people and followed that characterization with the interesting comment that "more guts" should be shown by junior faculty members on the campuses. He said they had an obligation to support their college presidents, and that they should insist that colleges be halls of reason, not halls of violence. If the heads of universities had such support from the junior faculty, they would be able to exercise much better control over the campus scene. But the alliance between the junior faculty and the student rebel movement had turned out to be incendiary, the President said.

Turning back to the war, the President told his guests that he knew very well that he could easily win lots of popularity by ending the war by Christmas—and bear in mind that this means Christmas 1970. He recognized the obvious: this kind of peace, one might say peace at any price, was what the country seemed to want, and it seemed to offer to him an easy way out. But he believed that if he were to take that easy way, the United States could never go to the help of any ally—Israel, Germany or any other—because we could not let down one ally without letting them all down. We could not pick and choose between allies. He added that he had not become President of the United States to witness the liquidation of all of our alliances and to see us lose our place of primacy in the hierarchy of nations.

All of this very serious talk was then interrupted by an odd incident, to which, as it happened, I was a close witness. In the seating arrangements, I was placed just down the table from the President, with Arthur Burns on my left and an otherwise unidentified Isidore N. Cohen on my right. I later learned that, along with his brother, Mr. Cohen was one of the principals of Joseph H. Cohen & Sons, a men's clothing manufacturer. They have offices in New York, and their primary plant in Philadelphia. The two brothers had recently sold their company to a big conglomerate, Rapid American, and so had become large stockholders in a large concern.

Reacting to the President's request for questions, Mr. Cohen got to his feet, as he put it, in an attempt to find out "what's going on in this country." Mr. Cohen's question, if that is what it was, turned out to be a 10- to 12-minute speech on the subject of his own opinions. They included an indictment of the Administration for its failure to act more vigorously; the bad advice given to the President by Dr. Burns and others about what was really going on in the economy; and a large helping of recommendations in a wide range of fields.

The moment was at first entertaining. Then it started to become quite uncomfortable. But the President took it good-naturedly, and, even though the other guests were squirming, and clapping to drown out Mr. Cohen, he refused to silence the man. He let Mr. Cohen speak his piece through to its end. A couple of times I surreptitiously reached out and tugged on Mr. Cohen's coat to get him to sit down—without much result.

When this incident had run its course—to everyone's great relief—the President picked up where he had left off. He told us that it would be very easy for him to clamp on price and wage controls and, more or less at the same time, to abandon Vietnam. But he believed that controls then would do more harm than good, and in a somewhat similar vein he believed that a sudden withdrawal from Vietnam would hurt too—particularly, it would hurt our ability to contain other aggressors. In that context, he seemed to be referring specifically to the USSR and to China; and he added that he would never see our ability thus limited while he was President. (Not until almost a year later was the President's intention to visit China announced.) At 11:05 P.M. the meeting broke up, to considerable applause. The President marked the occasion's end with a wry remark to those New Yorkers present that since they had missed their plane they might as well relax—a reference to the fact that the last plane leaves Washington for New York at 10:00 P.M.

At this distance from the event, I judge it to have been an important success. The *Wall Street Journal* the next day carried an article indicating that the guests were not at all enthused by what the President said, continued to be disturbed about the domestic impact of the Cambodian action, and were not really satisfied or gratified in any important way. My own judgment is different. I believe that the reaction was not so clear or simple as that, and on the whole considerably more favorable. I would say the consensus came closer to being this: that the President had diagnosed both the foreign and the domestic situations accurately; that with some time and a modicum of luck, his policies would succeed. I came away most impressed with his insistence on the fixed character of the Cambodian withdrawal date. He gave similar emphasis, with similar impression, on his determination to get the troops back from Vietnam on schedule.

On the way back on a charter flight—I was given a lift by John Loeb of Loeb, Rhoades & Company—I mused over this remarkable evening. One firm conclusion I came to was the sincerity of the President and his seven advisers. I could not and do not believe that the whole affair was just an elaborate show. The President did not shade the truth or try to force upon us any falsely optimistic prognostications. He was, after all, not only addressing a group that would be instrumental in spreading the information disseminated at the meeting throughout the country, but also he was talking to people with whom he would surely have to have future frank exchanges.

Of all the events of the evening, the most direct balm applied to the worst wounds of those present was administered by Dr. Burns. I did not know at the time, although I suspected it, that the Fed was in the process of increasing the money supply. Later publicly expressed confirmation of this impression was welcome news because it persuaded me as well as others that, in time, the bond market would turn around. I judged from Burns' comments that the mistakes of 1966 and 1967, when the Fed suddenly pumped so much more money into the economy, would not be repeated. Thus a compounding of inflation would be avoided, I thought, and a more orderly economic development could be expected. By mid-June, some evidence that this general interpretation was correct came to hand. The specific substantiation, as we have seen, was the rise in bond prices. And by the fourth quarter of 1970, there were glimmers of an upturn in the economy.

The White House dinner got its due share of publicity in the following couple of days. Once again Robards of the *New York Times* did a good reporting job in his account of the dinner in the Sunday edition, an account which included the menu—lobster cocktail, a white table wine, beef Wellington, a Chateau Lafitte Rothschild 1962, and coffee.

Of course, the verdict that the affair had been well worth its sponsorship was not unanimous. Philip Greer, writing in the *Washington Post,* complained that more heads of mutual funds should have been present, and he criticized the guests for telling the President not how things really were, but what he wanted to hear. Greer went on to say that "five will get you 10 in Wall Street that first, the dinner had nothing to do with the stock market rally and second, that the rally is a speculative bubble that will soon be just a memory."

Greer seemed to me, and still seems to me, to have been wide of the mark in this analysis. I respect him as a hard-hitting reporter, but in this instance I thought he was wrong. Indeed, I discussed the point with him and indicated my dissent at a luncheon some time later. My own judgment, as I've indicated, is that the dinner did mark a turning point in the stock market decline—that the idea was a good one, that the results were good, and that a line of communication was opened up which could have general value to the investing public and indeed to the economy as a whole. Of course the President can always go on television and speak to the nation, or call a press conference and be widely quoted. But the reception given such public signals by businessmen is quite different from the way they react when the signals are delivered, in the classic phrase, "live and in color."

While the President obviously cannot speak with great frequency to groups of business leaders, the fact that he did so in a moment of crisis strikes me as terribly important. Misunderstandings and garbles were pretty much ruled out by the means he chose. The general purpose of good communication was well served. Wall Street was in a crisis at the time, and a good deal of it had to do with Government monetary and fiscal policy, as well as with the war. The discussions dispelled some fear and clarified some thinking.

As I mulled over the importance of an understanding, or, if you like, even a tentative working partnership between Washington and the business community, the importance of good communication struck me more forcefully than ever. Naturally, my interest centers around individual shareholders, that being the strength and the primary concern of Merrill Lynch. Beyond the fact that 31-million individual Americans own stock lies the more significant fact, as a perceptive *New York Times* reporter wrote, "investors have become a potentially more powerful political force than ever before." It does not seem too farfetched to assume that these shareholders, who as yet have not clearly staked out a political identity, may someday do so.

They may, in the words of Donald Schwartz, a law professor at Georgetown University, become "surrogate for all citizens." Schwartz goes on to say that "this is the great potential in shareholder democracy. It will require a big shift in attitudes, but shifts in attitude are the products of education and communication." Americans affected directly and indirectly by the stock markets—through share ownership, pension and retirement plans, insurance policies, mutual funds, and other investments—form the largest single constituency in these United States. But until recently they have also formed one of the most completely forgotten. Within the past two years Wall Street and Washington have suddenly awakened to the political reality that investors are voters—and that they can be very angry voters when they believe their interests are neglected.

The arrival of the era of popular capitalism coincides with the coming of a new era of public skepticism and militancy. As fast as the number of investors grows, equally fast grows the number of consumers who complain. It is no longer sufficient to proclaim devotion to the public interest. The public now demands, quite rightly, performance in the public interest. Of all industries, the securities industry is perhaps uniquely vulnerable to the consequences of leaving the customer unsatisfied. For the basic capital of the industry is public confidence in the markets and the market makers.

Over the past two years, as we've seen, that confidence has been severely shaken. The effect of the shock waves passing through Wall Street and registering on the political seismographs in Washington has been to push market makers and lawmakers to recognize the importance of forming a new partnership to protect the interests of the investing public. Some form of collaboration, obviously, has existed since 1933 and 1934, when the landmark securities acts were passed. At that time the Congress wisely resisted the clamor for the government to regulate the securities industry in detail as retribution for the speculative excesses and dishonesty of the 1920s. Instead, the lawmakers adopted the principle of self-regulation, entrusting the exchanges and industry organizations with the responsibility for writing their own operating and financial rules and policing compliance by their members. The Securities and Exchange Commission was assigned the responsibility, among others, for supervising and ultimately enforcing *effective* self-regulation.

Under the stress of radically changing conditions and the inadequate response to change within the securities industry, the terms of the collaboration are shifting—precisely how much and toward what new balance of power and responsibility, it is now impossible to say. On his first day in office, the first SEC Chairman, Joseph P. Kennedy, spoke a blunt warning to his former Wall Street colleagues that still applies: "Times have changed and things that seemed all right four or five years ago are now out of the picture."

The new partnership, if one can so characterize it, will be what both sides work to make it. If the parties display wisdom, maturity, and farsighted responsibility (not their foremost characteristics in the past), free and competitive capitalism will be strengthened through reform, and public confidence fully restored. If, however, cooperation breaks down, ill-advised "reforms" may weaken the market mechanism, and we may wind up with what the late economist Joseph Schumpeter described as "capitalism in an oxygen tent."

Like so much else in American life, the relationship between Wall Street and Washington is a complex, many-faceted mixture of change and continuity. At one level, where headlines tell of woe and recrimination, the relationship appears troubled—and it is. At the working level of the marketplace, where most of the activity is reported in agate type, the relationship appears harmonious—and it is. (Merrill Lynch alone buys and sells more than $100-billion worth of Government and Federal agency securities each year—see table page 64.)

As the vast expansion of the Government securities market illustrates, the inhabitants of Wall Street and Washington, like Americans generally, have a talent for adjusting to unimagined situations in a practical and pragmatic way, inventing new means as new needs arise. But the talent for coping, for absorbing novel demands into the mainstream of continuity, is merely the bright side of another, thoroughly American trait. This is our tendency to remain preoccupied with immediate concerns almost until the moment the need for drastic change ("crisis") overwhelms us. It is not good enough to continue entrusting the future to luck and ingenuity. Too much is at stake. Moreover, crisis-driven reactions permit choice only among available alternatives, not necessarily the best ones.

The central question in our society, Peter Drucker reminds

us in *The Age of Discontinuity,* is, "What do we have to tackle
today to make tomorrow?" Applied to the partnership emerging between Wall Street and Washington, the question is, what
must we—market makers and lawmakers alike—tackle now
in order to insure strong and healthy popular capitalism tomorrow? The first thing we must do, it seems to me, is begin
closing a communication/information gap that yawns like
Grand Canyon. Hence I approve most heartily of the White
House initiatives I have just described.

The brand-new institution, the Securities Investor Protection
Corporation (SIPC), whose birth I have already mentioned,
has as its purpose to insure customers against the failure of
their brokers, up to a limit of $50,000 ($20,000 in cash) for
each account. Considering the cliff-hanging circumstances in
which it was created, SIPC so far has proved a useful and
workable institution—a better one in fact, than the creators
had any right to expect. For throughout the months of dash-
ing back and forth between Wall Street and Washington, it
was obvious that everyone concerned was operating in the
dark, uncertain of the most basic facts of the situation, except
that they were grim and urgent. It was a subject of speculation,
for example, just how many brokerage houses were in danger
of failing, and therefore the size of the risk SIPC would face.

Actuarial data were nonexistent, and the schedule of premiums merely guesswork. Senator Harrison A. Williams of
New Jersey, chairman of the Securities Subcommittee of the
Senate Banking Committee and like Senator Muskie a key figure in the creation of SIPC, came away from the experience
with some definite opinions. These were expressed in a candid,
thoughtful address to the Investment Company Institute in
April 1971, and are worth quoting at length:

> We in the Congress know far too little about how your industry
> works. Despite past studies there is a devastating lack of pre-
> cise information concerning the exact condition of the securities
> industry and the causes of the problems which it is experi-
> encing. To make changes . . . without knowing their effect
> could well bring about the very event we have so arduously
> worked to avoid: a major financial disaster on Wall Street.
>
> Each time the Congress has considered a specific reform . . .
> we were told by both the SEC and industry representatives that
> the immediate institution of such a reform, needed as it might
> be in the long run, could cause the failure of large numbers of
> broker/dealers. This in turn would accelerate the deterioration
> of the securities industry and cause a further loss in investor
> confidence.

Neither the SEC nor the industry has been able to provide the Congress with the necessary specific information for the enactment of sound reform legislation. This is true simply because the information is not available. To obtain facts necessary to make sound legislative judgments is the sole objective of the study which I am about to undertake . . .

Studies of Wall Street by the Congress and the SEC and others will soon help provide the accurate information indispensable to successful partnership and sound reform. But there is more involved in closing the information/communication gap than assembling and analyzing data. After the studies are completed and reports published, the same gap could eventually reopen, inviting another crisis. The exchanges and other self-regulatory bodies, the Securities and Exchange Commission, and the Congress should be continuously linked in an expanded and modernized information system, so that the Federal overseers of the financial community are brought closer to significant developments there.

Some improved means of communicating current data will have to be devised because the fact of geographical separation (and its psychological consequences) hampers the oldest and best human information system—face-to-face talk. Unlike their counterparts in such world centers as London, Paris, and Tokyo, American leaders of finance and politics go about their professions in separate capitals. They are denied the daily opportunity to rub elbows—and ideas. They live within quite different climates of opinion. They read about each other's activities in the newspapers, which, by their very nature, filter out much of what's happening because it is "routine." Yet awareness of the other fellow's workaday routine is the first step to understanding him, his accomplishments, and his problems. Information seems to flow only when the system *stops* working well.

Now, it cannot be claimed that men with different interests and perspectives, merely by talking and listening to each other, will automatically agree. Very likely they won't. But the chances of one's taking the other by unpleasant surprise are greatly reduced and so are the misunderstandings that arise from rude awakenings. Through the late 1960s, the Wall Street–Washington relationship was essentially one of benign neglect—not to say blissful ignorance—on both sides. We have seen how prosperity concealed the shakiness of poorly capitalized and badly managed firms from men in Washington who weren't paying close attention anyway. When the winds of adversity brought these structures down, the lawmakers were surprised—and they, in turn, surprised inattentive market makers by proposing stringent measures to shield the investing public from the storm.

Of course, there may have been no way to avoid the crisis of 1970, regardless of how often and how candidly financial and political leaders communicated. Too much had been allowed to go fundamentally wrong. But the lack of communication inevitably generated an atmosphere of suspicion, and belated cooperation began in a setting that had overtones of confrontation. As the Securities Investor Protection Act was moving to final passage, the Governors of the New York Stock Exchange sent a telegram to New York's Senator Jacob Javits: "We assure you and your colleagues of our cooperation in a spirit of constructive reform." Nothing less than that assurance would satisfy the industry's critics, who had seen too little evidence of such a spirit earlier.

Wall Street will have to make the psychological adjustment required to cooperate with Washington in good season and bad alike. This means shelving old prejudices and abandoning the wish that government would go away—except, of course, when it is needed. The government is in the securities industry to stay, on terms still to be decided. Acceptance of that reality is the premium the industry paid for its $1-billion insurance policy from the U.S. Treasury.

Perhaps the key to the adjustment required on the part of Wall Street is to expand its definition of professionalism. Men who are preoccupied with the short-term, often the minute-to-minute, fluctuations of the markets may perform well *as* capitalists, yet poorly *for* capitalism. Longer-term trends, particularly political trends, may have critical impact on the nature, strength and freedom of the markets, and time spent analyzing these trends is time well spent professionally. Any insight gained into future investment opportunities is an incidental bonus, as those who anticipated and profited from the rising concern for the quality of the environment can attest.

Wall Street can go a long way toward closing the information/communication gap, but Washington has its part of the bridge to build, too. Even if data were flowing as the Congress desires, there is reason to doubt that the lawmakers and the SEC as now staffed could handle it. Outmoded ideas and narrow preoccupations flourish also in Washington.

One day in the early summer of 1970, Representative John Moss of California, a member of Congress deeply involved in the creation of SIPC, performing with seriousness and solid competence, spoke to a visitor off the record about "the whole business of legislating and its frustrations." With the authority of long experience in the Congress, he singled out the chronic shortage of staff personnel as "perhaps the greatest burden of the legislator and the biggest obstacle to good legislation." He had only one full-time assistant and three part-time assistants, he said. "Yet I must deal with agencies every day that come into the hearing room with four or five times the staff I've got. So we all have to look to industry for some of the expertise. Yet, they have their own special point of view and you know that, and you watch that. Nevertheless the industry can be very helpful because they can give you the facts."

The Congressman closed his reflections with a pair of conclusions beyond argument: "It is long past time that Congress recognized the need for competent, comprehensive staffing. It's time the press and public stopped laughing about our complaints and started helping their representatives do the kind of job people expect them to do."

Since 1934 the Securities and Exchange Commission has been responsible for overseeing the performance of the industry's self-regulatory bodies and for keeping the rules of the marketplace up to date. In recent years the SEC has fallen woefully short of its capacity to meet these responsibilities. "We seem to have lost confidence in the SEC," Congressman Emanuel Celler of New York declared during House debate on the SIPC bill. ". . . When we say the SEC will do this and that, I wonder what indeed the SEC has been doing all this while. If the SEC had been doing its duty, we would not have this sorry state of affairs." Similar misgivings and complaints were expressed on the Senate floor.

True enough, the SEC too often moves very slowly or not at all. Delays in important studies and rule-making decisions are measured in years. In part, however, this reflects the stepchild treatment the SEC receives from the negligent Congress. Although the SEC is grossly underfunded and understaffed, each year it remits to the Treasury revenues from various fees and charges that amount to almost as much as its budget. In fiscal 1969 the SEC actually turned in to the Treasury amounts larger than its total budget—in business terms, it made a *profit*. But Wall Street and the investing public pay dearly for this survival of old-style economizing into the age of the computerized marketplace. Perhaps if the very modest fees were increased, Congress would be more inclined to give the SEC the funds it urgently needs to expand its staff and modernize its operations. Merrill Lynch, for its part, would be pleased to support an increase in SEC fees.

So there are obvious shortcomings in Washington's end of the partnership, which the Congress alone can repair. And there are obvious temptations to take shortcuts, which should be resisted. One of these is to bestow more power and authority on institutions unable effectively to use what they already possess. The SEC needs a thorough overhaul, yet one of the commissioners recommends simply installing a much bigger power plant in the same Model T. "If there is any lesson that has been learned from our experiences over the past few years," he declares, "it is that the Commission must have plenary power to take whatever action is required in the public interest and should not have to wait and see what action a self-regulatory body will or will not take before it acts."

In spite of the sorry evidence in support of that view and the undoubted concern for the public interest inspiring it, I would question whether the "lesson" is that clear-cut. Or whether putting more responsibility on Washington would make Wall Street a more responsive and constructive partner. On the contrary, it might so enfeeble the principle and practice of self-regulation that the markets would pass into the oxygen tent owned and operated by the government. Then the dynamic force of popular capitalism might flicker out. The whole burden of self-regulation and government regulation needs to be examined, weighed, and parceled out differently. The assignments of the National Association of Securities Dealers (**G**), the Stock Exchange, the SEC and SIPC must all be redefined.

Senator Williams, in his speech quoted above, acknowledged that Congress, over the past 37 years, "has never really undertaken a careful review of the self-regulatory procedures embodied in the Securities Exchange Act." His study and others are correcting that oversight and will recommend reforms to strengthen the foundation of the Wall Street–Washington relationship. It is the crucial assumption, always subject to being proved anew, that the market makers will make and faithfully obey rules serving the public interest. In 1969–1970 faith in that assumption came dangerously close to collapsing among investors and lawmakers.

Self-regulation fell into deserved disrepute because of Wall Street's self-made problems in two areas that I have discussed in detail and at length: operations and finance. Excuses, some rather plausible, can be made for the operational lapses of the securities industry, which, after all, experiences extraordinary fluctuations in its level of business. It isn't the easiest business to manage or plan on a long-term basis. But the financial irresponsibility revealed by the bear market was inexcusable. Too many of those engaged in the business of handling other people's money clearly didn't regard themselves as businessmen at all. Capital supposedly "invested" in the business was here today and gone tomorrow.

To enforce its rules, the New York Stock Exchange would have had to push distressed firms to the wall, compel liquidations, and expose customers to the hazards the Exchange sought to avoid. So as we've seen, the Exchange relaxed the interpretation and enforcement of its net capital rule. The hope, as the Exchange said in a special bulletin to members, was that if it allowed such firms to continue to operate, under closer surveillance "pending a scaling down of business and reduction of paper work backlogs," their liquidation would be "manageable." It was an awkward position, to say the least, and it proved to be an untenable one. The financial problems of the industry were too deep and fundamental, and the deficiencies in detection and monitoring safeguards too glaring, for such rescue operations to be adequate. By asking for emergency assistance from Washington in the form of SIPC, the industry tacitly admitted that the existing system of self-regulation, temporarily at least, had broken down.

The principle of self-regulation was sound and viable, but it had not been rigorously applied. Only under the spur of crisis did the SEC bestir itself. In 1970, for the first time in six years, its inspectors visited the New York Stock Exchange and checked on the enforcement of minimum net capital requirements for member firms. Some firms were required to file regular—even weekly—statements of financial condition. Firms were told to stop hiring salesmen and start hiring more clerical help to get paperwork unclogged. Highly individualized bookkeeping methods, which blurred the overall picture of the industry's condition, were ordered scrapped and replaced with a uniform system of accounting. (The system is not yet installed. The legal fight may go on for years.) These and other intrusions on management prerogatives were widely resented, but such pressure was necessary, and the self-regulators took the cue. "A few months ago, no governor [of the New York Stock Exchange] would have thought it proper to pry into the operations of a competitor," an SEC official told a *Wall Street Journal* reporter. "Now they're right down in the bowels."

So the Big Board tightened up its "early warning" rules on the debt-capital ratio of member firms, set up its special monitoring committee which directed emergency measures to prevent major failures, and launched the reforms I've explained aimed at strengthening the capital structure of Wall Street. Among the most important were the new rules governing the terms and duration of investment in brokerage houses, and the aggregate indebtedness permissible in relationship to capital. The main thrust behind such reform may be summed up just as concisely: capitalism is striving to regain its vitality, competition is being practiced and professionalism is being accepted. Wall Street may actually be becoming what Wall Street formerly claimed it was.

Truly competitive and professional market makers have less to fear from consumerists and Government officials than they do from colleagues who, contemplating reform, would rather sink comfortably into the oxygen tent. The decisive tests in the evolving partnership between Wall Street and Washington are likely to occur *within* the securities industry itself, between those who see what must be done *now*, today, to prepare tomorrow's free central marketplace, and those who see only today's trades and let tomorrow take care of itself. The outcome will determine whether the industry deals with Washington as a full partner, accepting responsibility, or a supplicant, accepting its fate.

Meanwhile, the SEC and the Congress, as overseers of change, ought to be undergoing simultaneous modernization that will permit them at least to stay abreast of the restructured securities industry. It is not clear that they will. Other regulators, such as the ICC and the FTC, have not found it easy or done conspicuously well. The pressures of competition and technology fall lightly, if at all, on the Government, and political pressures will not automatically bring a response attuned to novelty and change. On the contrary, competitive and modernizing forces in the securities industry could encounter stiff resistance from entrenched bureaucrats allied with the industry's stand-patters.

I am confident that this will not be the case, for Congress, in approving SIPC and placing the Treasury in a new role vis-à-vis the industry, clearly committed all concerned, including itself, to reform. All the musty corners should be swept clean—in Wall Street, the SEC, and the Congress—and the regulators as well as the regulated should cross the threshold of change. Whether the SEC would be more efficient under a single administrator, rather than its present five-man board; whether committee staffs should be expanded and professionalized; whether committee and SEC budgets should be increased, and by what amount—these are questions for the Congress to answer. What is important is that the lawmakers, when querying the market makers, see that these questions are also on the table. The new partnership between Wall Street and Washington should be an alliance of equals: men equally bound by the interests of the public they separately serve; and equally determined to apply their specialized talents to the common objective of expanding the prosperity of free men through free markets.

CHAPTER IX

The Shape
of the Future

CHANGE MIGHT BE DESCRIBED AS EXPERIENCE IN the present tense. In that regard, of course, Wall Street—and almost everywhere else for that matter—is always changing. But, as you have seen, the experiences of Wall Street during those three days in May were surely unique, and they have brought extraordinary consequences. It takes some knowledge and some attention—again, as you have seen—to appreciate what really happened on those three days. Fully to explain them has taken us both backward and forward in time—backward to some of the Street's history, to some of its practices, and to the roots of many of its methods and problems; and forward to the immediate improvement that followed the crisis, the high volume and good profits of 1971, and the present moment as the Street, like the rest of the country, awaits the outcome of Phase Two, which followed the 90-day freeze. Now, however, I should like to look further ahead—to the new skyline of Wall Street that will gradually emerge over the next five to ten years. What will the Street look like? What will it be like to work there? And what can the 31-million shareholders, whose numbers will swell to 50-million by 1980, expect in the way of services?

Basically, the radical changes will take place in two areas—environmental and organizational. From those two changed fundamentals will spring a thousand other changes, for you cannot alter the root without altering the branch, nor alter the branch without changing the leaves. I believe we can look forward to a Wall Street that relates much better to its customers; a Wall Street that ceases to think of itself as a club, or as a place where big money can be made quickly; a Wall Street where the most influential hand is no longer the dead hand of the past.

In a sense, although obviously not in a geographic sense, that means there will be no Wall Street—it will be replaced by a central market, held together by electronic communications, keeping its records in core memories, offering across the nation equal services and guided by evenhanded regulation. In recent years, lots of credence has been given to the notion of a moneyless society; I believe that the concept of a society without stock certificates will be realized first. In short, it is my judgment—reached not without some sentimental tinge of regret—that by 1980 Wall Street will have lost lots of its distinctive flavor. But it will also have lost its dubious reputation; and it will look and act much more like other conventional American businesses. On the whole, that will be good for everyone—except perhaps for the journalists, for I believe that the change will make the Street a harder place for a reporter to cover. In journalistic terms, the Street will be the scene of a lot less colorful action than we have witnessed in the past few years or even decades. Of course we who work there shall never be dehumanized, but our foibles are likely to show less, and the conduct of our business is likely to be less influenced by them.

My view in that respect is surely shaped in part by what I see around me today at Merrill Lynch. The colorful and highly individualistic era of Charlie Merrill is not likely to come again, especially now that Merrill Lynch is a public corporation. A partnership has secrets; it may keep those secrets for years. A public corporation has certain confidential information—it is likely to keep that only for moments.

Gradually, then, the Street will change, bent—perhaps not with full knowledge of the reason—on correcting the conditions that made the horrendous year of 1970 possible. Early to go, I imagine, will be that decorative piece of paper whose trips from buyer to seller and back again gave so many Wall Street managers nightmares during 1970: the stock certificate. If you have come along with me as far as this, I'm sure you know what it is—a not so lovely but very elaborate engraved piece of paper that seems a holdover from the Victorian and Edwardian ages (see footnote Chapter VI, p. 99).

The certificate states clearly what it actually stands for—capital stock, common stock,. preferred stock, and so on. Also, its par value is stipulated on the certificate. The stock certificate bears the signature of either the chairman of the board or the president and the company's corporate secretary. The registrar and the transfer agent, usually banks, are also named. The bank serving as registrar actually keeps the names of the shareholders to whom dividends are paid; the bank acting as transfer agent, on the other hand, actually does the day-to-day deleting of the names of those who have sold the company stock, and tacks on the names of those who have purchased it.

The reverse side of the stock certificate contains legal language, probably unread even by lawyers, as well as a place where the owner of the stock must sign before its ownership can be transferred. Once the stock certificate is signed, and the signature is guaranteed, it is negotiable—which means not just that its ownership can be legally transferred, but also that it has become suddenly a document worth the market price. To add to the general confusion, stock certificates come in various sizes, which makes them difficult to store and handle. That flood of business in 1968 that I have mentioned in so many different contexts meant also a flood of paper, an avalanche of stock certificates. It was the movement of these unwieldy pieces of paper, bouncing around the country like a squash ball around a four-walled court, that hit the Street so hard.

There are a considerable number of methods of improving the ways in which stock certificates move, and indeed some of these were put in effect following the chaos of 1968 and the results of 1970. But essentially, such improvements are like putting patches on a leaky water pipe. Eventually the pipe has to be replaced—the certificate has to be eliminated completely.

One of the interim steps along this road being taken by a committee known as BASIC (Banking and Securities Investment Committee) was formation of a joint committee by banks and brokers to work on the whole thorny question of the stock certificate. Initially, BASIC's view was that the certificate could not be eliminated, either quickly or perhaps ever; instead, it turned its attention to the feasibility of machine-readable certificates of uniform size, similar to the punched cards used in data processing. An immediate and as far as I know still unsolved problem in moving toward such a certificate is that no machines have been built that can read them fast enough to process high volume; but members of the committee are still looking into this, and encouraging some developmental research.

To appreciate the complexities here fully, you must understand what the stock certificate stands for and what it does. As evidence of ownership, it has existed since the beginning of brokerage. Individual purchasers of securities have become accustomed to looking on their certificates as the indisputable evidence that they got what they paid for. Many of them are not going to surrender that material comfort willingly.

The stock certificate's position, however, is entrenched for other reasons than psychological. Under the banking laws of most states, banks are forbidden to lend money on securities unless the stock certificate is put in their hands at the time they make the loan. This is not a matter for discretion on the part of the banks' officers—they either have the certificate in their hands, or they cannot legally make a loan on it. The same is true for other fiduciaries; executors of wills, and so on, are obliged by law to inspect the certificates themselves, and, in the old phrase, to accept no substitutes. Further, in the course of the transfer of the ownership of the certificate, which I sketched briefly in Chapter VI, many accompanying slips of paper—receipts, stock powers, legal documents such as power of attorney, copies of wills, and court orders—go along with the stock certificates, and much now-vital record keeping is dependent upon the certificate. As I said in a speech in 1970, "The stock certificate has more offspring than a Delaware shad."

So, when we consider this change, we must understand that it is far-reaching. Certainly legislation at the state level virtually across the country would be required. Furthermore, it may very well be that the Congress also would have to act before the stock certificate could be dropped overboard, thus lightening Wall Street's burden. Indeed, I have long had in mind that the only way such a reform could really be launched is by Presidential action—the appointment of a Presidential commission that would examine the desirability of eliminating the stock certificate, declare in favor of that goal, and then assume responsibility for encouraging all the necessary changes throughout the various levels of government. That kind of high-level and persistent attention to the matter is probably an essential prerequisite to ridding us all—banks, brokers, and public—of the stock certificate. No matter what the market value of the shares it represents, the stock certificate itself is too expensive. We cannot continue to pay for it.

One encouraging analogue can be found in the checking system. Not very long ago, bank checks came in many sizes and shapes. But that variety was engendering all kinds of confusion in the banking system. Therefore, representatives of the system concluded that checks should be of only two sizes, and that they should use magnetic inks so that they could be read by machine. Such a transformation was initially costly to individual banks, and some of them were opposed to it. Finally, however, the Federal Reserve Board took a hand. It imposed a penalty on any bank that did not use checks with magnetic ink, and it gave all banks one year in which to convert to the new system.

Under this threat, banks, which sometimes are passing slow, moved with unusual celerity. The deadline was met; the new system was put into effect within a year. The banks that had stood in opposition had cited as one of their arguments the probable unfavorable response from their customers; the fact is, however, that bank customers barely noticed the change. Today no one objects to the size of the checks or to the fact that they all have magnetic ink and code numbers on them—most people are not even aware of it. I see no reason why the same kind of improvement cannot come about with stock certificates.

Yet it is also possible that this evolutionary stage of standardizing certificates could be skipped entirely. Once the proper legislation is passed industry could move directly to computer printouts. After all, at present everyone with a bank account gets such a printout—his bank statement. Occasionally, individuals may have arguments with what that printout says—but no one challenges the general validity or usefulness of the concept. No one insists that he should be able to go down to his bank and look at his money, kept separately in a Plexiglas box. His bank statement satisfies him that he does own the cash that the bank says he owns and that the bank has the cash when he wants it. He accepts, and institutions accept, and the law accepts, the Simon-purity of that bank statement. There seems no reason why the same could not be done with stock certificates. The customer would receive a computer printout—a monthly statement—from his broker, which would serve as his evidence of ownership. Transactions would be shown on the statement. Appropriate back-up systems would operate much as they do with bank statements.

Had Wall Street in the early '60s seen what was coming and been working toward diminishing the importance of or eliminating the stock certificate, it would not have been so hard hit in 1970. And those who survived would be millions of dollars richer. It is too easy simply to say that on a busy Street in a busy town, it was too much to expect that the lethargy of many different interested parties, on a prosaic matter, could be overcome. What happened was also too much to expect—but it did happen. Lethargy can be lethal.

At present, and I hope the development will stand as evidence that something has been learned from the flood of 1968 and the drought of 1970, the New York Stock Exchange has in effect a Central Certificate Service (**G**)—and a Clearing Corporation (**G**). This service permits brokers and some banks to transfer securities among themselves in a manner much less cumbersome than the old method. Under the old system, if it can be so described, people known since the beginning of time as "runners" carried securities from broker to clearinghouse and picked up securities going from clearinghouse to broker.

Now, however, under the CCS, the transfer is made by bookkeeping entries. Brokers deposit large numbers of certificates with the CCS. At present Merrill Lynch has about $8-billion worth of stock certificates stored in the vaults of the Central Certificate Service. The Central Certificate Service "nets out" transactions at the end of every day. That means that it computes how many shares of U.S. Steel, for example, Merrill Lynch bought or sold for customers in the course of a single day, and it figures out with how many other brokers belonging to the New York Stock Exchange Merrill Lynch was involved in these transactions. At the end of the day Merrill Lynch's position in U.S. Steel is adjusted on the books in the Central Certificate Service to reflect the movement in that stock. Assume that Merrill Lynch has 60 trades in U.S. Steel in a single day. In 20 of these trades, assume that Merrill Lynch was the seller on behalf of its customers; on the other 40, it was a buyer, also on its customers' behalf. Postulate that the 20 selling trades totaled 2,500 shares; the 40 buying trades totaled 3,500 shares. That means that, in balance, as far as Merrill Lynch is concerned there was a net change of only 1,000 shares. Instead of having to tote to the clearinghouse certificates whose total number of shares came to 2,500 for delivery to other brokers, and to take away from the clearinghouse 3,500 shares to bring back to its vaults, Merrill Lynch can simply "net out": its position on the CCS "blotter" stands at 1,000 shares for that particular day.

Assuming that none of Merrill Lynch's buying customers wanted to keep the certificate itself and that all of the selling customers had kept their certificates stored with Merrill Lynch, there would be a minimum of bookkeeping and transfers. If half of the buying customers wanted their certificates, Merrill Lynch would have to arrange with the transfer agent to have 20 new certificates issued. If half its selling customers had formerly had their certificates in their own possession, then they would have to deliver them to Merrill Lynch. We would have to accept them from whatever office was concerned around the country, ship them to New York, then forward them on to the transfer agent. Certificates would then be voided, and the names of the former owners removed from the book.

The presence of the CCS obviously restricts a good deal of the movement of the stock certificate—what is becoming known as "immobilizing" it. However, if there were no stock certificates at all, we would be still better off. A printout of one of Merrill Lynch's computers would advise the transfer agent to add 20 new holders and delete 10 old ones. At first, this printout would probably be delivered by hand; later, compatible machinery might do the job.

The benefits of computerization go further than segregated securities. (Earlier, I explained that fully-paid-for securities are kept segregated by the broker, under penalty of law.) While a broker must keep fully-paid-for securities separated from all others, he does not actually possess and put aside stock certificates bearing the name of each individual owner. He holds those securities in Street name in bulk. For example, the books of U.S. Steel as of September 1, 1971, show Merrill Lynch to be in possession of 200,-000 shares. However, none of this is in fact owned by Merrill Lynch. It is probably owned by some 4,000 to 5,000 different customer accounts. But Merrill Lynch holds only one stock certificate, or only a few, which total 200,000 shares. When U.S. Steel declares a dividend, it sends only one check to those 5,000 shareholders—one check made payable to Merrill Lynch for the total amount of dividends due on all the shares. Merrill Lynch collects that check, and in turn breaks it up into the 4,000 or 5,000 separate amounts—crediting each shareholder with 50¢ a share, if that was the dividend declared, for each of the shares he owns. So, in this example, the stock certificate really serves no useful purpose.

Once a customer was in possession of his broker's statement, he would have all the evidence of ownership he needed to prove that his dividend had been paid to him. Should broker or bank have to ascertain whether the individual was in fact still the owner of the shares listed on his broker's statement, a quick query to the transfer agent could be made by machine. This would involve no further advancement of the electronic data processing art. Indeed, it would be precisely the same system used by reservation bureaus of airlines when they seek to determine whether seats are available on a given flight. Also, the result of the elimination of the stock certificate would be more security, not less: there could be no theft or loss, no mutilation or destruction.

So the goal seems both highly desirable and attainable, needing only top level intervention, the imposition of a couple of reasonable deadlines, and the threat of penalty if the deadlines are not met. Once in effect, the certificateless society will change Wall Street remarkably. Many boring clerical tasks will be done away with, to be performed by machines; the people thus freed can be retrained and then employed in jobs that enable them to use their minds and energies more profitably. The easiest analogy that comes to mind is the automatic elevator. All former elevator operators are not unemployed. They are doing work that is more worthy of a man's capacities.

Modern electronics will bring more changes in our industry than the elimination of the stock certificate, despite the enormous importance of that single accomplishment. There is promise in other areas as well. The "registered representative" (**G**), whom we call an account executive at Merrill Lynch, may have as many as 500 to 600 active clients. During the course of the ordinary working day, he may very well talk to as many as 50 of these. And he is asked an enormous variety of complicated questions—about companies and securities, about the merits of one investment versus another, about general movements of the economy and the market. And he is also often asked about the latest bit of news that may have come over the Dow Jones ticker, so that he needs to be not only informed when he settles down to his work in the morning, but in touch with what is going on in the financial world during the day. In a single day, he is required to produce a wide variety of information. At the same time he is being informed from a great many sources, including the Merrill Lynch newswire—which is very inclusive, transmitting some 75,000 words every day.

Currently there are 1,600 stocks listed on the New York Stock Exchange. Another 1,025 are listed on the American Exchange. Probably 10,000 or more are traded in the over-the-counter market. In addition, all kinds of bonds are floating around—United States Government issues, Federal agency issues, corporate bonds, municipal bonds, foreign bonds—

and all of them have many, many subdivisions under those generic headings. Any client could ask any question about any of those items. We have some pretty smart account executives in Merrill Lynch, but no matter how smart he is, no one can know it all—in that sense, regardless of his individual intelligence, the account executive is likely to be pretty inefficient as a transmitter of information.

But his intelligence plus the memory core of a computer is something else again. With the proper data-processing systems at his disposal, the account executive can pass his client's question on to the machine and get an answer in milliseconds. That answer can be transmitted to him either on a printed page, in what is called "hard copy," or on a video screen. Just as every account executive now has a machine that gives quotations on listed and unlisted securities, he will soon have available a screen that can tell him much more. By hitting the proper code on a keyboard in front of him, the account executive will be able to summon up just the information he needs, and pass it back quickly to his client. This might involve such complicated matters as moving averages, future earnings projections, the past history of multiples, bond yields, the desirability of tax-free bonds given certain tax brackets, elements of securities versus elements of risk, and so on in infinite number. And at some point—I have no doubt this will come about—the screen will also contain live data; that is, the news will no sooner have happened than it will be up there for the account executive if he wants it. The account executive's productivity will thus be increased.

Such voluminous information available so speedily would serve little purpose, at least from the point of view of the broker who is in business to make a profit, unless it could be translated into orders. And the system now employed for entering orders on the floor of the New York Stock Exchange ranks just a little bit ahead of the old Morse telegraph, which was used to transmit orders from branch office to New York headquarters in the early 1900s. In the '40s, when the Morse system finally went out, its place was taken by teletype machines, whose teleprinters have since become faster.

Right now, messages go through electronic switching systems from branch offices directly to the floor of the Exchange or to the home office of the broker. The messages usually need not be rerouted from the home office to the floor. But the method of processing orders also will soon be overtaken by electronic change. In today's brokerage office, orders are taken somewhat in the same manner as sales slips were handled in the department store of the 1930s. The account executive takes an order from his customer, and sends it to an order clerk in the same office by pneumatic tube. Then the complicated transmission of the order, already described, begins. But in the future—some part of this has already begun—the order will go to the floor of an exchange directly from the desk of the account executive, through the same type of keyboard system he will be using to get information.

This kind of trade will of course revolutionize all the related operations of the industry. Machines, rather than people, will keep track of orders and will detect errors—one hopes much sooner than they are detected now. For example, if the customer wants to buy 100 shares of stock selling at $55, and by error the order comes out reading "buy 100 shares at $35," the machine will reject the order and return it to its originator. Erroneous orders will thus not be transmitted to the floor. Such a data-processing system can be adjusted so that it has tolerances—let us say of 10%. In the example we have just given, the computer can be keyed to reject orders to buy when they are under $50, or orders to sell when they are above $60, on the theory that these orders are so far from the current market price that some mistake must have been made by the sender.

If, however, the order is open—that is, if the customer wants his order held until such time as that particular stock sells at $48 and then executed—the computer can make such an entry. If the stock in question is one that fluctuates widely, the tolerances can be increased to whatever seems reasonable—perhaps to 20%. New orders would then be accepted when they are not more than 11 points or so away from the $55 price.

With electronic guards, computers can also monitor a customer's account. If a customer puts in an order to sell 100 shares of a security, the computer can confirm that he is in fact their owner. If he is not, no sale could be made; the order would be rejected on the basis that an error had been made in its initiation.

My guess is that errors in the transmission of orders or in their execution in 1969 probably cost Wall Street close to the enormous sum of $100-million. Computers require large investment, but the industry will get the investment back, with good return, once it moves ahead into the electronic age.

Nor are brokers the only ones who will benefit from savings

by electronic communications. Once a modern network is set up and operating, brokerage houses will be able to establish offices in communities smaller than any that at present can support such offices. Thus the reach of the industry will stretch to include people who are now unreachable because they live too far from the larger metropolitan centers. Brokers have ventured into small communities from time to time in the past, but they have almost always withdrawn as soon as volume dried up. With better communications, we can look forward to many more outlets for a retail firm—smaller branches than any we know today, with fewer chairs and sofas, but with better machines giving quotes, supplying information and recording trades. This would ultimately increase the number of capitalists in the capitalistic system.

When all this electronic gear is in place, will we still need a New York Stock Exchange? Probably not in its present form. But still, I think the notion that a battery of computers in Omaha, Nebraska, perhaps vaguely resembling the computers that now constitute the Strategic Air Command, replacing the floor of the Exchange, is a bit far out. The specialist on some floor somewhere, despite his current fears, will in my judgment still have an essential role to play in the transaction process.

Right now, the specialist (**G**) on the floor keeps what is called a "book." The book contains a list of brokers who want to buy securities at prices lower than the current market and those who want to sell at prices higher. If a broker gets an order to sell at 50 a stock that is currently trading around 54, he takes that order from his telephone booth on the floor of the New York Stock Exchange and carries it to the specialist's post (**G**). There he puts the order in the hands of the specialist for execution. In his book, the specialist logs the broker's name and the selling price. If the stock comes down to 50, and a buyer comes around, the specialist carries out the order and sends the broker a report. Hours and weeks could elapse from the time of the original entry to the execution.

At one time, much was made of the privilege of getting a look at the specialist's book. The theory was that the book contained some pretty clear indications of which way the stock was going to go. However, the relationship between book and stock price—assuming it existed—was the reverse of the one you would assume would pertain. I noticed many times during the '50s and the early '60s that when the specialist's book was crowded with orders below the current market for a stock, the price of the stock would go up and the orders would never be executed. Conversely, if orders were bunched above the current level of the market, the market would go down and the stocks would never be sold. It always seemed that the short-term run of the market went against the sizable build-up in the book. I was never able to determine why this happened and never able to get a specialist to explain it to me. But, as a result, brokers were left with a lot of unexecuted open orders—something like the beach after the tide went out.

Open orders on the books require a good deal of the specialist's time and attention. Also, at Merrill Lynch we review all open orders daily, and contact our customers to remind them of their open orders every three months. After a certain period of time has gone by, the orders left on the books may begin to look ridiculous—a buy order of $20 for a stock currently selling at $70, for example. And open buy orders (as well as open sell-stop orders) have to be changed whenever a stock goes ex-dividend, when there are mergers and so on. This entails a lot of bookkeeping for both broker and specialist.

In recent years, the books have become thin. There are now far fewer open orders than there were 10 years ago. The explanation is found in the impact of institutions on the market. Institutions now make up over 55% of the total trading on the New York Stock Exchange, and they do not enter open orders. So the specialists' books are remarkably light relative to the 1950s.

And I expect that they will become lighter still. The fact is that the book could now be replaced by an electronic machine. Computers could record open orders and run tapes of all transactions. Furthermore, the computer could be programmed to act when the value of a stock changes: that is, if a stock falls from $55 to $50 a share, the computer could automatically alert the specialist that his outstanding orders at $50 were ready to be executed. It could give him a printout of all such orders and their size. After execution, the specialist could send reports of the transaction back to the originating broker, also by electronic means. This would free the specialist from having to watch all transactions; no orders would be lost; easy verification would be at hand.

There is yet another improvement possible. If a stock normally trades at around $55 per share, a specialist could program his machine to indicate his willingness to buy or sell at that level with a quarter of a point spread. For example, on a market quote of 55–55 1/4 the machine would execute an order to buy 100 shares at 55 1/4, the offering side of the market; it would also execute an order to sell at 55, the bid side of the market. The program could be further refined to provide that after 400 or 500 shares have been executed at the same price, the machine would change the price in the direction that the orders were running. If there were more buyers in the market and a total of 500 shares or more were executed at 55 1/4, then the machine would move the offering price up to 55 3/8 or 55 1/2. This would follow the normal sequential pattern on the floor of the Exchange.

Under those conditions, a large order could still change the tone of the market for a particular stock, as it does now. If the specialist suddenly found that he was confronted with an order to sell 3,000 shares in the midst of all this buying, he would take over from the machine and use his judgment from that point on. The machine could simply be instructed to disregard its program until further notice. Then the specialist could decide how best to handle the 3,000-share sell order. Perhaps he would buy it all at 55 or lower. Perhaps he would offset it with some open buy orders on his book at 54 7/8. In any case, the human factor—the judgment of the specialist—would be critically important at this juncture, and it would also be available—it would not be diluted by the trivial and mechanical functions that now occupy so much of a specialist's life. Under the conditions we are discussing, the specialist could put the program on the machine back into effect whenever trading resumed its normal pattern, or he could continue to intervene himself for as long as he thought necessary.

With the market price as determined by the specialist's book being in fact posted by computer, buy and sell orders arriving at the specialist's post simultaneously could in many cases be executed without the specialist's services. As orders were executed, market changes and price adjustments would be recorded in the memory of the machine. The machine would adjust its prices in the same direction that the market was moving, and adjust its program to take activity into account.

All this obviously leaves an important function for the specialist to perform. But still, once the volume on the New York Stock Exchange was being handled by one of the gigantic computer systems—IBM, Univac, Control Data— obviously a lot less activity would take place on the floor of the Exchange. There would probably be fewer specialists, each of them specializing in a longer list of stocks than they can manage now with their archaic record-keeping systems. Some of them, in the language of labor, would become "technologically obsolete." But no changes of the magnitude I have been discussing can come without some fallout. The machines taking over would make fewer errors, and would be less expensive in the long run. An area almost three times the size of a football field would be replaced with relatively small offices, plus space to house computers. The Exchange itself thus would become a gathering point where specialists would meet around a print-out machine and apply their services where they are needed.

Even those specialists willing to accept this somewhat reduced function might be impelled to argue that it would be only a holding operation—and that the end of their profession is in sight. They might say that the 3,000-share order which I have just cited could also be programmed into a machine, and that no human element need ever intervene. Of course no one can say what the long-term outcome of electronic data processing will be as applied to the stock exchanges, nor at what point "progress" will cease. But in my view when you approach orders of the size of the one I have used as an example, the element of judgment becomes all-important. As an investor, I would prefer to have specialists handle such a trade, and I believe that when substantial amounts of risk capital are involved, people will have to take over from machines. In that sense, the marketplace is always going to be what the Stock Exchange was under the buttonwood tree in 1792 or, for that matter, what the Roman Forum was in the heyday of empire—a place where people meet. I don't believe that human element will ever be eliminated.

Some form of the changes I have been discussing is already in being in microcosm. And it grew out of the least organized, most disparate, and most decentralized market of them all— the over-the-counter market. In early 1971 this market began to operate under a new system called NASDAQ—the National Association of Security Dealers Automatic Quotations. Designed for the NASD by Bunker-Ramo, a division of Martin Marietta, this NASDAQ system had a gestation period of around three years. It was carefully studied by various committees of the NASD, by that body's board of governors and by groups of outside engineers. In a truly revolutionary development, NASDAQ has remade the cumbersome system of trading that marked the over-the-counter market since before the Civil War.

Fully to understand the nature and importance of this

"counter revolution," some familiarity with the history of the over-the-counter market is necessary. In its early years in the mid-nineteenth century, the over-the-counter market's principal activity was the buying and selling of municipal and corporate bonds over the counters of private banking institutions. Later, it became a place where all kinds of securities that were not listed, and therefore not traded, on the major exchanges of the country could be bought and sold. The term "unlisted" later became synonymous with the over-the-counter market, but this is not technically correct, since the over-the-counter market is not the only place where unlisted securities can be traded. But the over-the-counter market does provide a trading market for unlisted securities, which would be far less liquid if no such market existed. While no one knows what the pre-NASDAQ volume of the trading conducted on the over-the-counter market was on a nationwide basis, there is no question that, if bonds are included in the calculation, it greatly exceeded that of all the national exchanges combined. Right now, with NASDAQ on stream the daily volume for common stocks is less than that on the New York Stock Exchange, but much greater than the volume on the American Exchange.

But until the revolution came, the over-the-counter market labored under some serious disadvantages. Because of its scope and complexity, quotations were not available on the basis of last sales or of opening transactions. Each over-the-counter security is quoted on the basis of a bid price and an ask price. The bid is the per-share amount at which the stock can be sold, and the ask is the per-share amount at which it can be bought. The difference between the bid and ask prices is "the spread"—and that, of course, is what interests the people who make the market operate. While some of them are brokers, far more are dealers—that is, they are market makers who take positions in a stock and buy for and sell from their "inventories." They are, in short, usually principals and not agents—in the parlance of the street, dealers and not brokers. (At Merrill Lynch, the customer is charged the regular commission rates whether Merrill Lynch is a principal or an agent.)

Obviously, in a market made mostly by dealers, some special protection for the customer is required. In the past, the protection was supplied by means of three separate inquiries made by whoever represented the customer of three separate market makers in order to determine whose price was best, before the transaction was executed. In theory anyway, and probably for the most part in fact, the customer's agent went where the price was best. But special care was required where the customer's agent, his broker, was also a market maker in the security that the customer was seeking to buy or sell.

NASDAQ has changed all that. To begin with, it is just what it says it is—a quotation system. The old method of having the broker telephone to three dealers in an effort to seek out the best price has been done away with. Instead, the broker has a video screen in front of him, and by operating a keyboard, he gets information from, or adds his own input to, the state of the market.

NASDAQ is an electronic marketplace on three levels. The first level is its simple provision of information. By punching the keyboard, the broker can get on his screen a display showing the median bid/ask prices for any stock on the over-the-counter market. That means, of course, the median set by all the market makers. The second level, intended more for the retail trader than the retail salesman, shows not only this median price but also the individual bids and offers for any particular security made by all the market makers. The list is presented in descending order, starting with the best bid or offer. Finally, the third level is intended only for the market makers. It permits them to put in changes of their own quotes. These latter changes, however, are revealed only to other market makers; the information is confidential between brokers. Only brokers can make changes in prices—they have a special device on their machines for this purpose.

To the individual customer, the electronic change that NASDAQ brings is fraught with meaning. It means that quotes for some 2,500 counter stocks are continuously updated as market conditions change. Brokerage firms can use their terminals to determine without delay the entire spread of bid-and-ask quotes entered by all market makers in any security used in the system. The broker, and therefore of course the customer, will go to the dealer who is making the best market. And the market will not fade as quickly as the over-the-counter market has in the past, when, in down markets, many dealers "pull their bids," or, in other words, simply reduce their prices. NASDAQ has a surveillance system making it quickly apparent which market makers are strong and staying in the market, and which perform only when they decide it is profitable to do so.

The NASDAQ system also promises to bolster public confidence in another way. One of the great deficiencies of the market in unlisted stocks—or, to put it the other way, one of the great strengths of the New York Stock Exchange and other exchanges—is that transactions on their floors are made public. NASDAQ holds out the possibility that this strength can be added to the over-the-counter market. If the NASD were to pass a rule that every broker who sold stock on that market would have to report his transaction and the price at which it took place, the computer's core memory could record the transaction and make it available in a printout. This, in effect, would put transactions in the over-the-counter market on a tape comparable to the tape of the New York Stock Exchange —those moving numbers that you see in every brokerage house. NASDAQ has already assigned a symbol to every over-the-counter stock, an essential preliminary to the publication of a tape (and a monumental job in itself). So the next stage is well within reach and would mark further progress in one of the greatest assurances that can be given to the investing public, that is, the assurance that trades are publicly recorded —that no over-the-counter trades are taking place under the counter.

A wind that blows up so much change is bound to upset somebody. In one sense the new methodology of NASDAQ constitutes a challenge to the New York Stock Exchange. The Big Board's rules are very detailed about circumstances under which its members may trade in the third market—the market in listed securities made by nonmember firms off the floor of the Exchange. These rules have been under attack for years, but the attacks until recently have been successfully fended off. Now, however, the advent of NASDAQ has very much increased the danger that the third market will grow at the expense of the New York Stock Exchange. Thirty stocks listed on the Big Board (as well as one on the American Exchange and two on the Midwest Exchange) were initially quoted through the NASDAQ system. More have been added since. Suddenly, third market quotes in those stocks have become just as accessible as quotes on the floor of the New York Exchange. And just as suddenly, it has become evident that the third market prices are sometimes just as good as and sometimes better than those prices quoted by the Exchange. A few large third market houses, led by Weeden & Co., have been trading in listed securities off the Big Board, and evidently with some success. The volume of trading in the stocks quoted by NASDAQ and also listed on the Big Board has increased since NASDAQ began. But whether this increase is caused by the fact of the NASDAQ quotations, or by some other factors—

one may be that most of these stocks are of the kind that big institutions were accumulating in the period following the initiation of NASDAQ—remains to be seen.

The broker's fiduciary responsibility is of key importance here. If U.S. Steel is trading on the floor of the New York Exchange and is also listed on the NASDAQ system, the broker in principle at least would have to check both markets before he executes a customer's order—that being part of his duty to get the best price for his customer. At the moment, while this practice is probably being followed, NASDAQ does not list so many of the New York Stock Exchange quoted stocks as to cause a major shift in the direction of trading. But as the number of such stocks increase, that time might come, and it may be troublesome for both specialists and brokers.

The day when some kind of merger will be made between the makers of the third market and the New York Stock Exchange may also be hastened. In his report and recommendations prepared for the New York Stock Exchange in August 1971, William McChesney Martin Jr. proposed such a merger. (I served as one of his advisers, but the report was his own.) If that eventuality does not come about, the SEC, which has allowed the third market to grow without much control or scrutiny, will have to step in. Formerly, the SEC was able to argue that there was not so much activity in the third market as to warrant continuous surveillance.

But now the situation has changed radically, and the likelihood is that third market activity will continue to increase. Thus the need for more regulation is going to become daily more acute and the regulatory bodies must govern equally. Two separate systems, especially when they deal in the same securities, cannot exist side by side unless the regulatory hand is equal for both. Petulance accounts in part for the third market's unregulated growth, but the time for petulance has passed. Hard feelings between the SEC and the New York Stock Exchange must be put aside, in the spirit of collaboration that I have discussed in the preceding chapter. Indeed, in a sense that spirit of collaboration is the most radical change of all that must come. There is no assurance that all else will fall into place if it does come; but it is certain that nothing will fall into place without it.

CHAPTER X

The Meaning
of Conflict

GRANTED THE BEST SPIRIT IN THE WORLD ON THE part of both the regulators and the regulated—and that is quite a grant—I still believe that the most important regulator of all is competition. At present, Wall Street is hiding behind a protective pricing system, while it preaches free competition and free markets. As I mentioned in a public speech, that is like catching Carry Nation tippling in the basement. We say that competition is good for everyone. We base our investment advice on the competitive stance of the company we are analyzing. The price of a stock is set by the forces operative in the marketplace. Yet we live with this anomaly of a fixed rate structure. We live as exceptions to our own rules.

For years, we permitted this price-fixing to continue as a minimum structure. Now the SEC in certain applications is saying that the rates should be maximum as well, thus snuffing out all competitive light. I don't happen to believe that lawyers in Washington know what the right price is for our services. I don't know how they could know what "right" is, or when "right" changes.

Prices are arrived at by a study of costs and a mark-up for profits. Prices change as costs rise or fall, and as the demand for the product or service changes. They react to new efficiencies, to inflationary or deflationary pressures. That's the creed. Wall Street must learn to live by it. Despite the fears, chaos won't result. The commission charges for buying and selling bonds on the over-the-counter market operate freely right now. Nobody charges the New York Stock Exchange minimum any more. The system works perfectly well. Bond traders aren't getting rich, and the customers aren't getting skinned. So I suggest that in stock trading as well we recrown the customer king. Let's offer servants truly competing for his favor.

The most significant means by which the force of competition will make itself felt will be free pricing. The fixed commission structure led to the erosion of what was once the central market, as well as to the rise of a free-wheeling and secretive third market. Freely competitive rates will do a good deal of centralizing for us; fixed rates will mean fragmentation. It is clear, as I testified before the SEC late in 1971, that the industry would not be ready for competitive pricing if it were announced now to become effective next Monday morning.

But we must move as rapidly as is feasible toward this goal. An interesting move would be to free rates for trades under $10,000 as the next step, rather than continue to lower them slowly from the high end of the scale. We now have competitive rates only for trades over $500,000, on the theory that experience at this level will indicate to us the effect of these rates on institutional trading, and so help us to determine the future shape of the marketplace. Why then should we not have competitive rates for trades of $10,000 and under, to give us new experience and to prepare the way for action based on that experience as well? Indeed, a powerful argument can be made that it is precisely such new experience that we need, rather than more experience of essentially the same quality and character on the upper end.

In this connection, according to the New York Stock Exchange, despite the fact that competitive rates are in effect for trades over $500,000, the firms that were the largest executors of those big transactions before have not become larger still since. The much-feared economic concentration has not taken place. I doubt that very much of it would take place if rates were totally freed. Some mergers would probably come about—but when you consider that the typical securities firm does $2-million a year in securities commissions, and has about four branch offices, you may conclude that a little merging is not a dangerous thing. I think it would be healthy.

But the competitive environment will always allow for the presence of smaller firms. Specialty houses that have special relationships with clients will always be part of the brokerage business. No one firm will ever be best at everything. Small firms with special talents in any one of a number of directions in this complicated industry will not only survive, but will thrive. This is not to say that we will always have 4,500 broker-dealers in the country; the total number may indeed be reduced. But I would expect a reduction of relatively modest proportions, not a drastic shake-out that would leave only half a dozen giants facing each other. The richness and intricacy of this industry is such that a pattern of that kind would not serve the customer well, and thus in my judgment is unlikely to emerge.

At present we have a new commission structure. And we are well into Phase Two of the President's economic program. Rather than preventing us from moving toward a competitive structure, these two developments give us ample opportunity to move in that direction with all deliberate speed. The new structure will meet the current undeniable need of the industry for an increase over the 1958 price levels. And Phase Two, about whose outcome I am personally optimistic, gives us a proper climate in which gradually to feel our way toward the radical change that will come. Phase Two is a time of testing and watching for the whole economy. It can serve very well as a testing time for the securities industry also. To use the new rate structure and the environment of Phase Two as excuses to postpone indefinitely the changes that we so badly need in pricing would be hypocritical. Ultimately, the therapeutic shock has got to come.

The response that such a suggestion will bring goes like this: it's easy for Merrill Lynch to come out for competition. You're the biggest in the industry. What about the small firm?

There are several answers to that. First, if all firms have to be the same size before we make a change that is so logical, and so obviously good for the customer, then the change will never be made. It may be too bad that we can't all start out as equals in a new game. But as a practical matter we have to move ahead from where we are.

Second, the securities industry serves millions of customers, from the mythical Aunt Jane with five shares of AT&T to the Prudential Life Insurance Company with its billions of dollars in assets. The customers have needs as diverse as shoppers in food stores. Some want to buy by the case. Others buy by the ounce.

With prices being set by free forces, some brokerage houses will be hurt. That's undeniable. But they are being hurt now, right through the protective armor of fixed rates. Those who serve a true economic function, who see a need and fill it, will survive. Specialty stores won't go out of business.

And the public at large will benefit. I cannot make that point more clearly than it was made in the report of the

Council of Economic Advisers early in 1971. I quote the passage.

> In a competitive market, if a private company uses productive resources inefficiently, market forces should force it to relinquish them. This is one of the reasons why we should rely as much as possible on the discipline of the marketplace to protect the public interest. . . . Regulations devised for an earlier economic environment can stifle innovations and new developments in today's market. . . . Regulations often prescribe or support minimum or maximum prices . . . the problem is to make certain that "fairness" in setting rates does not put an umbrella over inefficiency, and that "soundness" in financial institutions does not become a pretext for impeding competition and innovation.

Besides bringing competitive rates, the construction of a new marketplace, foreshadowed by the advent of NASDAQ, is sure to bring with it a reconstitution of the membership of the New York Stock Exchange. Such a remaking, one form of which has been proposed by William McChesney Martin Jr., has far-reaching implications. In another context I have noted that 55% of all the trading on the New York Stock Exchange is now done by institutions: mutual funds, pension funds, insurance companies, and so on. These organizations, with their professional management and vast resources, cannot be satisfied by the same brokerage services that satisfy the individual. Institutions are in business, after all, to satisfy a clientele of their own. As their influence and authority have grown, they have become more and more reluctant to pay to a broker the regular fixed commission schedules, and more and more outspoken about their desire, and indeed their responsibility, to make their transactions in securities at as low a cost as possible.

To ignore the fact that institutions are under pressure and obligation constantly to do better for their clients is to overlook one of the key factors working for change in our financial world. Institutions are subject to competition, not only from institutions of the same kind but from others as well. Indeed, financial institutions can no longer be neatly compartmentalized. According to the report of an important Presidential commission that studied the country's financial structure, the distinctions are going to become even less clear in the future. Life insurance companies sell mutual funds; mutual funds have purchased life insurance subsidiaries. Corporations may administer their own pension plans, but they have the alternative of turning to banks, which also manage such plans. Virtually every kind of institutional investor competes not only for the individual's dollar, but for the corporate savings dollar as well. In a kind of reciprocal thrust, the individual whose savings are turned over to an institution—either by him directly or by his company through a pension plan—has become more and more concerned with good performance. The more sophistication the individual acquires, the more pressure he applies.

In seeking to save on brokerage, big financial institutions, whether hybrid or not, have looked with growing interest and a sense of keen anticipation at the prospect of membership in the New York Stock Exchange. Thus far, such membership has been denied them. But the pressures have not ceased to mount. Consequently, these financial institutions have found other ways to accommodate those pressures.

The foremost example is the case of Investors Diversified Services, a huge, sprawling mutual fund and financial and insurance complex based in Minneapolis. IDS is controlled by a holding company, the Alleghany Corporation, which in turn is controlled by Allan P. Kirby, who ranked among *Fortune* magazine's 1968 list of centimillionaires. Once a railroad holding company, Alleghany has moved out of that unprofitable arena—it still has large holdings in the Missouri Pacific and other railroads—and into the more profitable business of managing money.

The relationship with Alleghany put a formal stop on the possibility that IDS might join the New York Stock Exchange. The Exchange's rules forbid membership by any subsidiary— the membership of the Exchange generally viewing the Exchange as a meeting place for brokers who are executing orders on behalf of customers. By that definition, obviously IDS is ineligible. A further refinement of the New York Stock Exchange's reasoning goes like this: the Exchange itself is responsible for the behavior and the financial soundness of each of its firms. How could it be responsible for the subsidiary of a sprawling conglomerate? No one could possibly know what the management of such a parent might do. The parent might go bankrupt, and so damage the customers of its subsidiary. The New York Stock Exchange might be in the essentially absurd position of having to guarantee not only the subsidiary over whose activities it had oversight, but also the actions of the parent—over which it would have absolutely no control. Further, for a member firm in the New

York Stock Exchange to be primarily manufacturing diodes, running retail stores or manufacturing shoes seems ludicrous. So the simple principle that members of the Exchange must first and foremost be brokers has been continuously asserted by the Exchange.

But IDS could not be frustrated in its basic thrust to save costs. It moved along a different path. It acquired Jefferies & Co., a brokerage firm that was a member of the Big Board and other exchanges. Jefferies resigned from the New York Stock Exchange (it is a member of the Pacific Coast and the Philadelphia–Baltimore–Washington exchanges) after it contracted to be acquired by IDS. Now Jefferies does not recapture commissions for IDS, but it does do a public brokerage business—presenting the New York Stock Exchange with a complicated issue and, at present, a complicated law suit. Meanwhile IDS does recapture some of its commissions through another subsidiary, IDS Securities Corporation. Thus the $6-billion complex strengthens itself—but a great deal of brokerage escapes the floor of the New York Stock Exchange.

In a similar pattern, more and more institutions are now tending to conduct their trading activities away from the floor of the Exchange. Their primary concern, as I have noted, has been the search for lower commissions. But, as with many other topics concerning finance, there are dovetailing motives. Institutions have also been interested in finding a market for large blocks of stocks that cannot be readily handled on the floor. One of the limitations of the specialist system that we have described in an earlier chapter is that the specialist, using his own limited capital, is often unable to take up positions in huge blocks of stock worth millions of dollars.

From the point of view of the members of the New York Stock Exchange, looking at potential new members, there is much merit to the argument that the Exchange is not intended to be a rebative mechanism. There is also some merit to the argument that subsidiaries of big institutions ought not to belong—ultimately, this could tie off commissions, the life blood of the Street. However, not all the arguments are on one side. Institutions point out, and rightly, that members of the New York Stock Exchange have long had their own mutual funds. Lehman Brothers runs the One William Street Fund; Dominick & Dominick, Drexel Firestone, Smith Barney, and Bache, among the major firms, also have their funds. Merrill Lynch owns a subsidiary, Lionel Edie & Co., which runs two mutual funds. At one time Dreyfus & Co.

controlled the Dreyfus Fund. So the institutions ask the obvious question: why should a member firm be allowed to control a mutual fund, when a mutual fund cannot be permitted to join the Exchange?

The New York Stock Exchange, however, has clung to its policy that the primary purpose of a member firm is to be a broker. That condition of course would rule out membership for mutual funds, since *their* primary purpose is to handle other people's money, and their objective in seeking membership on the Exchange is simply to get a reduction in the commissions that they pay. The Exchange, however, decided in 1968 that trades in such large volume were entitled to a volume discount—and a discount for trades of 1,000 shares or more was put into effect then.

That reduction in commissions represented the extent of the concession that the Exchange was prepared to make at the time. But later, again under pressure, the Exchange permitted competitive rates on trades whose value exceeded $500,000. While our experience with commissions for such trades does not permit any hard-and-fast conclusion yet, it is safe to say that the result of competition in this area has been to reduce commissions still further. According to the New York Stock Exchange, customers benefited by some $17-million from competitive rates on large trades during the first six months the new rates were in effect. Whether institutes passed on some of the savings to their customers, I do not know—I hope so.

However, exchanges did not all speak with one voice. The Pacific Coast Stock Exchange was less stringent in its requirements. The Midwest Stock Exchange and the Philadelphia–Baltimore–Washington Exchange permitted mutual fund management companies to join. Subsidiaries were also allowed to become members. Halsey Stuart, a leading investment banking firm, had been a member of the Chicago Stock Exchange—a forerunner of the Midwest. Halsey Stuart was acquired by Chicago Title. Chicago Title is owned by Lincoln National, a holding company for the Lincoln National Life Insurance Company of Fort Wayne, Indiana. Thus Halsey Stuart is not only a subsidiary, but a subsidiary of a subsidiary. Still, the Midwest Exchange, once it had permitted the admission of subsidiaries, could not balk at the double layer: Halsey Stuart remains a member of the Midwest.

Looking at the position of IDS and Halsey Stuart, the Philadelphia–Baltimore–Washington Exchange, whose ethics are often called into question by some of the older members of the

Wall Street community, really flung open its doors. The only requirement it imposes for membership is now a specified amount of capital. Even foreign banks are members of the Philadelphia–Baltimore–Washington Exchange today; yet American brokers are not allowed to join foreign stock exchanges, by rule of those exchanges themselves.

Still, the New York Stock Exchange continues its policy against institutional membership. Its position was considerably strengthened by the public endorsement given by McChesney Martin to the principle that institutions should not be permitted to join stock exchanges, but the Martin report has not settled the matter for all time. Until a national, cohesive, all-embracing, equally self-regulating market comes into being —and that remains a vision for the future—the fragmentation that results from the denial of membership to institutions on the New York Stock Exchange will continue.

There are risks no matter which way this complicated matter goes. But, looking ahead and trying to outline the shape of the Street 10 years from now, my judgment is that there will be some modified form of institutional membership on whatever kind of centralized exchange has emerged by then. This may take some form of associate membership: some means by which the big institution can operate its subsidiary without acquiring the full responsibilities of membership. Or, it may be that a simple arithmetical test will have to be passed: any member of the central exchange, whatever it is to be called, will have to do a public brokerage business, and will not be allowed to get more than half (or some substantial percentage) of its commission revenue from any single source. The SEC is said now to be favoring this kind of resolution.

My prediction is that the healthiest development would be just that one. Public brokerage should continue to be a prime requirement. But I believe that any institution that is primarily a dealer in securities should be allowed to join the New York Exchange. The days when the Exchange could be selective, and bar from membership such organizations as Blyth & Co., Weeden & Co. and similar institutions, are surely ending. That will mean more competition for Merrill Lynch. We will be engaged in competitive struggles with bigger and stronger opponents than we have known for years. Yet I believe that that too will be a healthy trend.

Still other aspects of this question need to be explored. Behind it lies the whole matter of the propriety of a broker engaging in the managing of money. It has been argued that the broker is simply the agent for the public customer who is buying or selling securities on the exchanges. For this service he receives a commission. But precisely because he receives a commission, he should not be allowed to manage the money of any client—since, so the argument goes, the broker benefits every time there is a trade, and his recommendation will surely be "buy" or "sell" and not "hold."

The same rationale, by extension, applies to underwriting. An underwriter of securities performs many useful and complex functions, but in this connection the essential function is the purchase of securities from a corporation and their sale to the public. This is the function of a dealer—that is, a principal, and not agent. The argument against the dual function runs like this: as a broker, the securities firm, probably a member of the New York Stock Exchange, conforms to Exchange regulations and receives the protection that membership affords. Part of that protection is membership in SIPC, which protects customers but also obviously helps brokerage firms, since public confidence is engendered through the resultant insurance. Exchange membership also brings with it the (to my mind) rather doubtful right and requirement of operation under a fixed commission structure.

But when it becomes an underwriter, a brokerage firm also becomes a dealer—and it is to some degree exposing all members of the community to risk. A custodian of securities and cash for his customers, a broker is endangering the security of his position by buying stock from a corporation. The Merrill Lynch prospectus, issued at the time we became a public corporation, put the matter succinctly: "Underwriting involves risk."

But I cannot accept the argument that the functions must therefore be separate. And, peering down the road to the kind of community we are going to have in 1980, the notion of separation becomes absurd. Underwriting is the essence of capitalism—the gathering from many places of capital for the use of corporations. In a community so many of whose functions are vital for the economy at large, this investment banking function is the most vital of all. Investment bankers, and that includes the investment banking divisions of brokerage houses, have raised the money-raising process to a remarkable degree of efficiency in the United States. Indeed, in an industry which in the course of this book I have characterized many times as archaic and even medieval, investment banking stands out as a conspicuous exception.

Through retail brokerage houses (and in this respect obviously I speak as a partisan) millions of individuals have invested in the stocks and bonds of thousands upon thousands of corporations. Capitalism has literally been spread across the face of America by this process. Many large companies have achieved geographic balance in their ownership, and have established good relations with large portions of the population and far better public understanding than they could hope for otherwise, as a result of the methods of investment bankers. To expect an underwriter to make a thorough study of the company he is serving—which he is emphatically obligated to do under SEC regulations—but not to sell its securities would be to divorce the responsibility for the merchandise from the retailer. That would enable both retailer and underwriter to point to the other as the responsible party should something drastic go wrong.

Far from separating the two functions, I think the future will bring them closer together than ever. And I believe it is in the interest of the organized, centralized, efficient and low-cost marketplace that I envision as emerging to encourage just this intimate association. Again, here I cite the opinion of Bill Martin, who in the course of his report showed great sensitivity to the matter of conflict of interest, even to the point where he suggested that brokerage houses should divest themselves of their mutual funds. But he showed no inclination to tamper with the present mechanisms of underwriting. Perhaps the enormous volume of money that the mechanism has raised so efficiently deterred him.

Underlying the debate about underwriting in brokerage is the more general philosophy concerning conflict of interest. The securities industry surely will have continuously to confront the charge that an inescapable and insuperable conflict of interest is inherent in carrying on brokerage and in managing money. It has been suggested that the two functions are totally incompatible, and that legal rulings, regulation, legislation—the whole familiar battery of weapons—are going to be required to separate them. That may indeed be what happens. But I doubt that it will. Logic is against it. Without entering into the particulars of the issue, permit me to lay down a few principles once again.

A life without potential conflict, in our interrelated business world, is like a business without risk—impossible to legislate, and of doubtful wisdom if possible. Congressmen and presidents live perpetually with conflict—between the public interest and the desire for reelection. The performance isn't perfect—but it isn't impossibly bad, either. But when one senator, pure in spirit, voted as his conscience dictated, even though he knew it would jeopardize his chances of re-election, the act was considered selfless enough to win him a full chapter in John F. Kennedy's *Profiles in Courage*.

And, if you will, look elsewhere. Newspapers and magazines and television, presumed exquisitely objective in their editorial judgments, are dependent on advertisers for the revenues that enable them to publish and to profit. District attorneys want justice and need convictions. Teachers want to stimulate interest in learning for its own sake—but they must publish or perish, too.

In short, if the road to hell is paved with good intentions, the road to heaven is paved with bad temptations. We cannot build a wall against every foible, against every unethical act, or we would be forever immobilized. Obviously, we need standards of conduct to govern this aspect of the securities industry, as we need standards for politicians and for news media and for education. But to rule on the matter without considering that brokers have always been money managers, that brokers also have a responsibility to give out information and disclose facts and pass judgments, and, in short, that life cannot be lived in watertight compartments, is to act naïvely or from ignorance. An easy platitude says that a man cannot serve two masters. I say that, in modern corporate life, a man who cannot serve two is unlikely to be hired by either.

The brokerage industry of 1980 will also be quite different from the present one in terms of the qualifications of those participating. The general raising of entry requirements that I and others in the industry have been urging for so long will surely have come about by then. We will have accomplished the study that the industry needs so badly today—a study that will reveal to us how we should set standards of entry, including professional managerial standards, for our industry. We shall almost surely have qualification by examination then, of a far more stringent nature than the rather inconsequential standards now in effect. Also, I believe that levels of required knowledge will gradually be lifted over the years, and that examinations given by the governing bodies will recur periodically. In many states a driver is obliged to have his car inspected annually and to pass a second driver's test after a certain number of years have gone by. That might be an educational precedent for our industry. As we have seen, many of the troubles that afflicted us came from the fact that as managers we were badly prepared for the volume of business that broke over the markets and over our heads from 1967 to early 1969. So the character of the whole community will change.

But surely the climate of the future will be refreshed by the clean air of more competition. Bit by bit, the industry's windows will have opened. The central marketplace, the certificate-less society, the electronically conveyed information and the electronically delivered orders, the modern specialists' book that is no book at all, the cheaper means of buying and selling stock that our ingenuity will surely devise, the ubiquity of the wide range of services now available only in the metropolitan centers—all this, I have said, is on the way.

Nothing could damage our industry more than to assume a retrograde posture at this juncture. To resist constructive change is to diminish and endanger vitality. To cling to outmoded forms is to write your epitaph. You may recall some of the movie stars of the 1920s and early '30s—Ramon Navarro and the other great actors and actresses—suddenly confronted with what was then a technological miracle: talking pictures. Many of them, it turned out, had voices that were perfect—for a silent screen. And when television entered American homes, lots of radio personalities were locked out. In short, old form and new mode clashed. The old form could not survive. But I believe that regressive tendencies can be overcome, and that the methodology of the securities industry can be altered to fit the new demands being made upon it.

In general, then, that is the shape of the future for our industry, and the shape of reforms to come. The long and difficult period from which we are now emerging will, if we learn its various lessons, have been a salutary experience for us.

There are several frames of mind, however, that we must forgo—whose luxury we cannot afford. We cannot be like the hypochondriac who is getting well and resents the fact. We cannot indulge in cheap optimism about the future—it will take hard work and good management to make it a good future for Wall Street. Disaster and near disaster make people conservative—and rightly so—yet we must be progressive and receptive to change. Let me suggest a familiar homily. In every old man there lives something of the child. This is continuity, and we have good reason to cherish it. But we do not expect an adult to suck his thumb all his life. The analogy is simple enough: we can keep part of the past with us. But we've got to dismiss what I can only describe as fear of growing up.

GLOSSARY

American Stock Exchange Price Change Index: The index is a measure of the daily average change in the prices of all the common stocks and warrants traded on the American Exchange. These changes, up or down, are computed at regular intervals throughout the trading day and are added to, or subtracted from, the prior day's index to obtain the level of the new index. The starting level of the index was established at 16.88 to coincide with the average price of all Amex common stocks and warrants on April 29, 1966. A new issue is added to the Index after it has been traded for one hour. At that point, the number of issues used as a divisor to compute the average price changes is increased by one. When a stock is removed from trading, it is also removed from the Index, and the number of issues used as a divisor is reduced by one.

Association of Stock Exchange Firms: The Association was founded as a voluntary, non-profit, unincorporated trade association with a membership of over 500 firms and individuals. Begun in 1913 as the Partners' Association, its members now account for 90% of the business transacted on the New York Stock Exchange, and represent the full reach of investment services to institutions and individuals, such as the purchase and sale of securities on the various exchanges and in over-the-counter markets, underwriting, dealing in corporate securities, municipal bonds, United States Government obligations, and the sale of mutual funds.

The ASEF has now merged with the Investment Banking Association (IBA) to form the Securities Industry Association (SIA). The merger is logical, since so many securities firms belonged to both groups. The SIA will have about 850 members.

Basis Point: This measure of the yield of a bond issue is made up of three components: the price, interest rate, and years to maturity. A bond, selling in the aftermarket above its original issuance price, will yield a number of basis points less than at the original price and vice versa. A basis point is 1/100 of a percentage point. Thus the difference between a yield of 7.05% and 7.10% is .05%, or 5 basis points.

Block Positioning: "Blocks" of stock—traditionally over 10,000 shares—are usually handled by institutional houses, which deal with large financial institutions rather than the general public. As there may be difficulties or delays in matching buy and sell orders for large blocks of stock, the institutional house may take all or part of the block for its own account and dispose of it later. This involves a degree of risk and ties up capital; but substantial gains can be made.

Here's how block positioning can make money for a firm. Let's say a broker obtains an order to sell 40,000 shares of a corporation's stock at 25. By finding a buyer for the 40,000 shares, the broker can earn a commission on both the buy and sell sides of the order. If the broker is able to find a buyer for only 30,000 shares, he may be willing to buy the remaining 10,000 shares himself. His commission for handling one side of the 30,000-share transaction will run upward of $6,900; that is the minimum commission for amounts up to $500,000. For the balance, where the commission is negotiated, perhaps the firm will pick up another $3,100. This gives the firm a total commission of $10,000 ($6,900, plus $3,100) for one side of the transaction, or $20,000 for both.

If the price of the stock drops, the positioner takes a loss on the 10,000 shares he owns. But he would still make a profit if the loss were less than the commissions earned on the 30,000 shares. For example, if the positioner takes a loss of 3/8 point on his 10,000 shares ($3,750), he would still show a gain of $16,250. If the stock goes up in price, of course he does better.

Bonds (Bond Markets): Bonds are certificates of long-term debt, priced to yield the investor a given amount of interest if he holds them to maturity. Unlike common stock, bonds do not give the holder ownership in the company.

Bonds bear a par value, a coupon rate, and a maturity date. A bond with a par value of $1,000, a coupon rate of 6%, and a maturity date of 1990 will provide the holder with a return of $60 each year until 1990, at which time the holder will also be repaid the face amount of $1,000. But the price of the bond will fluctuate after the initial offering, and a person who might later buy the bond in the open market at 90 (that is, $900) would obtain a return of more than 6%. In addition to the "current yield" of 6.67% per year ($60 as a percentage of $900) there would also be an additional return of the difference between the $900 cost and the $1,000 redemption value. In the example cited above, the "yield to maturity" would be approximately

6.98% per year. If a buyer paid more than par for the bond, his yield to maturity would be less than the coupon rate of 6%.

Box Differences: These are shortages (or overages) in the inventory of securities held in a broker's vaults. For a rough analogy, assume a woman places her fur coat in a storage warehouse at the end of the winter. If the warehouse is unable to locate the coat when she wants it in the fall, the difference is one fur coat. If it were a security left with a broker, such a difference would be called a "box difference."

Box differences arise when the securities in the broker's possession differ from the securities that his records indicate should be there. The reasons for a shortage could be an actual physical loss of securities through theft or for other reasons; a delivery of securities to another broker in excess of the quantity recorded; receipts of securities from another broker in an amount less than he is required to deliver; or errors in recording securities movements among various accounts. Overages occur when a broker has more securities on hand than his records indicate he should have.

Broad Tape: This is the term widely used on the Street to identify the Dow Jones newswire, a news service that prints the most important financial news, plus economic and political developments that could have a bearing on the stock market. "Broad" is used to distinguish the news service ticker from the stock ticker, which printed the volume and prices of security transactions on a one-inch-wide tape within minutes after the trades were made on the trading floor.

Over the years there have been many improvements in stock ticker technology. The old glass-domed ticker that printed 285 characters a minute back in the 1920s was replaced in 1930 by a 500-character printer, which, in turn, was replaced in 1964 by a 900-character printer.

Central Certificate Service of the New York Stock Exchange (CCS): A central depository for securities held by member brokers, CCS is designed to eliminate much of the costly, time-consuming effort involved in the physical movement of stock certificates held in Street names among firms. Transfers are effected by a simple entry on the books of the CCS rather than by actual movement of certificates.

On any given trading day a retail firm's customers may purchase perhaps $3-million worth of securities and sell only $1-

million of them. The firm then has to pay the Clearing Corporation the difference between the aggregate of the purchases and sales on the settlement date. Before that deadline, clerks from the firm must pick up the securities from the CCS and deliver them against payment to the bank designated as custodian. But the firm may find either that CCS does not have the stock available in the proper certificate denominations, or that the banks do not have the proper instructions to permit them to pay against receipt of the securities. In both cases, the firm has already paid the selling broker via the Clearing Corporation. In the first instance, CCS must send the securities to a transfer agent for the proper certificate denominations. This could take a week or more, leaving the firm without either collateral, or use of a portion of the $2-million, until CCS is able to provide the stock and the house is in turn able to present it to the bank for payment.

Clearing Corporation (of the New York Stock Exchange): This organization was established in 1920 to expedite and improve stock clearance procedures. A stock transaction includes the execution and clearance of an order. The execution involves the use of the facilities of an exchange to locate a seller or a buyer, and then to consummate the trade.

The clearance covers arrangements for the actual exchange of and payment for the stock certificates. After the New York Stock Exchange established its clearing facilities, the American and all other national exchanges set up similar facilities.

Commercial Paper: Promissory notes issued by a corporation on its general credit, commercial paper is simply an IOU. The rate of interest depends on the general credit of the borrower and the general state of the market. Commercial paper is usually of short term duration, typically 90 or 180 days.

The commercial paper interest rate is now the basis on which two leading New York banks set the rate they charge to their large, most credit-worthy customers.

Commission Charges (Rates): These are the fees a broker charges for purchasing or selling securities as a customer's agent. The New York Stock Exchange has fixed commission rates for transactions in stocks listed there, subject to review and change by the Securities and Exchange Commission. These fixed rates have generally prevailed on the floor of other exchanges as well. They are based on the number of shares and the amount of money involved, decreasing as these rise. The subject has become one of the hottest on the Street in recent years, with Merrill Lynch and now a few others opposing fixed fees and favoring competitive rates.

Cost Push Inflation: This rise in price levels is caused by increases in the cost of labor, materials, and other elements in the production process. These cost increases lead to higher prices, which in turn become higher costs for the buyers of these goods and services. Thus a spiral starts, even though there may be sufficient supply to meet demand.

Costs and Revenues Committee: This is a special committee formed in 1957 to develop proposals for rate increases. This work resulted in the increases that went into effect in 1958. The committee consists of 17 members and an executive secretary. The members are representatives of eight major firms, six of which are large houses, three small-to-medium-size retailers, two regional houses and four specialist firms.

Current and Constant Dollars: Current dollars represent the level of prices prevailing for each of the years specified, and are not adjusted for comparability with other years. Constant dollars are derived by dividing current-dollar figures by their corresponding price indexes based on a year specified as 100. They therefore provide a means of gauging true growth in the economy. The base price year currently is 1958/1959. On the basis of current dollars, the GNP rose in 1970, but on a constant-dollar basis it showed a drop.

Debenture: An unsecured, long-term certificate of debt, the debenture is, like commercial paper, a sort of corporate IOU. It represents a company's promise to pay; it is not backed by collateral or a mortgage.

Demand Deposit: These are bank deposits that can be withdrawn at any time by the depositor without prior notice to the bank. A regular checking account is the prime example. Normally no interest is paid on demand deposits; indeed, on any but large accounts, a service charge for the handling of the checks is usually levied. Member banks of the Federal Reserve System (that means all nationally chartered banks and those state banks that wish to join) are required to maintain reserves at their district's Federal Reserve Bank to cover a percentage of these deposits.

Demand Pull Inflation: This rise in price levels is caused when too much money bids for too few goods. The demand for goods is greater than the economy's ability to produce them, which forces prices up. This kind of inflation is distinguished from "cost push."

Discount Rate: The interest rate that the Federal Reserve Bank charges to its member banks when they borrow money, the discount rate has traditionally been the base of the rate that commercial banks charge their best customers. As the entry about commercial paper explains, this base is no longer used throughout the banking system.

Setting the discount rate is one of three ways the Fed controls the availability of money. Another is by fixing the reserve requirements (which must be held in cash or Treasury bonds) against demand deposits of commercial banks. The third is by the sale or purchase of Government bonds on the open market.

Disintermediation: This is the situation that occurs when normal financial intermediaries are short-circuited in the investment process. For example, people usually deposit their money in banks or savings institutions, and those organizations, in turn, make investments in corporate bonds, Government securities and other obligations with a portion of those deposits. (The balance may go into other loans and as mortgages.) In the period we are discussing, individuals withdrew their savings to invest them directly in bonds, thus disintermediating.

Dividend Differences: In a broker's accounts of dividends paid on securities of which he is holder of record, these discrepancies sometimes appear. Corporations pay their dividends in cash, or sometimes in additional stock. When the broker is the holder of record of securities owned by customers and left in his custody, he receives from the dividend-paying agent a check or stock certificate equal to the amount due on all the shares he is holding for his customers. Sometimes this amount may be more or less than it should be, and a dividend difference results. The usual reasons for these dividend differences are that the securities deposited with the broker have not been transferred into the broker's name, or that the broker or paying agent has inaccurate records of the amount of stock the broker should be holding.

Dow Jones Industrial Average: Originally a transportation average, the Dow Jones was made up of the stocks of 12 railroads, one steamship line, and the Western Union Company. It was first computed in 1884. In 1896 the Industrial Average was started, based on the closing price for each industrial. At first it was published only sporadically in the *Wall Street Journal,* but after a few months it began to appear daily. In 1916 the list was expanded to 20 stocks, and in 1928 to 30, the present number. Over the years, some individual stocks have been dropped from the list, and replaced by others. Custom and the emphasis given it by the *Wall Street Journal* have made the Industrial Average by far the most frequently cited of all indicators.

Big swings in just a few of those stocks that have great numbers of shares outstanding, such as General Electric or General Motors or AT&T, can influence the averages very markedly. But they may not reflect the actual course of most stocks on the market on that day. So you may frequently find that Dow Jones Industrial Average has gone up, but you may also find that on the same day more stocks listed on the Exchange went down than up.

You may also be distressed to find that stocks you own went down on such a day, and you may find it hard to take pleasure, therefore, in the movement of the averages. An old saw, heard much more outside of than on the Street, declares that "you cannot buy the Dow Jones Averages," but this obviously is untrue: you certainly can buy the stocks that make up the averages if you want to. Since there has not been a change in the composition of the 30 stocks since 1959, you would not have to do a great deal of trading, once you had "bought" the averages, to keep them. But are you willing to accept "average" performance?

Dow Jones also prepares an average of 20 transportation stocks, 15 utility stocks and a composite of 65 stocks.

Dow Jones Industrial Averages Close: This is the figure that goes down in the record books. The levels that the Dow Jones may reach, and then retreat or rise from, during the course of a trading day are not normally entered as records. At one point on February 9, 1966, the Dow Jones Industrial Average actually pierced 1,000 on an intraday basis, reaching that high point about midafternoon. But then it fell back a bit and closed at 995.15. So, in spite of that mid-afternoon performance, at this writing it is accurate to say that the Dow Jones has never reached 1,000.

Earnings Multiple: Also called the price-earnings multiple, this is the ratio of the price of a stock to its annual per-share earnings. If a stock earns $2 per share, and sells at $20 per share, its multiple is 10. When earnings are on a rapid growth curve, multiples are higher, which explains the prices of stocks like Xerox or IBM. When earnings level off or falter, multiples tend to come down.

Eurodollars: These are dollars like any other, but they are in circulation in Europe and elsewhere outside the U.S. and to some extent walled off there—at least in the sense that regulations of the Treasury limit American companies from exporting additional dollars. But since it is helpful to our balance of payments to have those dollars brought back, they can be repatriated. When interest rates in the United States reach high levels, or European rates decline below domestic rates, Eurodollars tend to flow back home.

Federal Funds: These loans made on an overnight basis by one bank to another help the borrower to maintain minimum reserves against deposits, as required by the Federal Reserve Board. Funds are constantly being shifted among the more than 13,000 banks, so that some temporarily have excess reserves while others have deficiencies. The actual transfer of funds is accomplished by debiting and crediting the respective accounts of the banks at the Federal Reserve Bank of the district. Thus, a bank borrowing Federal funds obtains an increase in its reserve balances for one day and pays the lending bank interest for that day only. The use of the word "Federal" in this term can be misleading because the funds come from private, rather than Government, sources. The word comes from the "Fed's" requirements.

Fed's Window: The facility of the Federal Reserve Bank for lending money to member banks is officially known as the Federal Reserve Discount Window. A member bank can go to the Fed and borrow money, using as collateral promissory notes of the bank's customers. Through the Window, the Fed can affect the money supply by setting the discount rate. It can shut off the flow of funds by "closing" the window.

Floor Broker: A member of the Stock Exchange who executes orders on the floor of the Exchange; the floor broker, unlike the specialist, who deals only in particular stocks, can execute orders at any post for another brokerage house. This means a lot of walking, and some floor brokers claim they cover as much as 15 miles a day.

Certain floor brokers are known as "two-dollar brokers." The term originates from the fact that $2 was once the standard charge the broker made for his brokerage services. Today the fee for floor brokerage ranges from $1.15 to $4.65 per hundred shares, depending on the price of the stock. In spite of the change in price, though, the term endures.

Fundamentalist: This securities analyst concentrates on a company's past earnings records, its present operations and its future plans, and relates those to the prospects for the particular industry and the over-all economy. Like technicians, fundamentalists believe they are getting back to first principles. But the fundamentalist, unlike the technician, takes the position that the graphs will start up when the earnings and the economy warrant, and not when the lines have gone in any one direction for a certain period of time. Among fundamentalists, analytic powers are crucial, since the better an analyst knows a company's management and capacities, the more likely he is to recognize a potential that will later be realized. But here again a thousand unforeseen events can interrupt what at the moment seems like the reasonable or likely course of events. Most good market analysts consider both the technical and the fundamental point of view in making their judgments.

General Partnership: In this association of two or more individuals as co-owners of a business for profit, all the partners are equally liable for the debts of the partnership to the full extent of their personal assets. A partnership does not pay a Federal income tax, although it must file a return. Individual partners pay personal income taxes on their shares of the profits.

Give-ups: These arrangements between brokers cover a variety of transactions, usually involving several parties. A member of the Exchange on the floor could act for another member, executing an order for him with a third member and passing on, or "giving up," the second member's name instead of his own; or a broker could handle a stock transaction for a customer who normally traded with another house and give the latter's name to the selling broker.

The transactions that have been more usually associated with the word—the giving up of a portion of a commission on large transactions by the executing broker in favor of another whom the securities owners may designate—have now been largely eliminated, as the New York Stock Exchange has ruled against the practice.

Gong: A bell over the floor of the Exchange is sounded to signal the opening and close of the day's business and to herald various announcements. Gaps in the archives of the New York Stock Exchange leave the gong's origins obscure; one of the few facts known for certain is that it has been sounded electrically since 1903. Before that it was struck by hand.

The gong sounds three times to signal the opening of trading; once to halt trading for announcements; twice to indicate trading's resumption. It is sounded continuously in the final 15 seconds of each day's trading. Sometimes the gong sounds to announce disciplinary action against members, or in an emergency. It was sounded to halt trading following the news of the fatal shooting of President Kennedy.

Gross National Product: The total national output of goods and services produced by the nation's economy, valued at market prices, is its GNP. The goods and services included are largely those bought for final use by private consumers and government, gross private domestic capital investment and net foreign investment. It includes allowances for depreciation and for indirect taxes, such as sales and excise taxes.

Haircutting: If all a firm's capital is in cash, it has 100% liquidity. But when firms put up securities as capital, the New York Stock Exchange permits only a portion of the value of those securities to be counted as true capital. Municipal bonds are now valued at 80% to 99% of their current price, depending on their rating and maturity. Common stocks are reduced in accordance with their quality—some may not be counted as capital at all. A firm that puts up $100,000 worth of common stock is, so far as exchange rules are concerned, credited with only $70,000 worth of capital. The reduction is called a "haircut."

As of July 15, 1971, an extra deduction of 50% of the basic "haircut" is applied to the market value of securities if the securities of one issuer form more than 15% of a firm's net capital. Interestingly, even though member seats on the Exchange have at times been valued at many hundreds of thousands of dollars, they cannot be counted as capital. Their haircut is 100%!

Hypothecation: This is the pledging of negotiable securities as collateral for a loan, while still retaining title to the securities. The practice of using securities as collateral. for loans had its beginning in Italy during the Renaissance. It later became common in eighteenth-century England. After the War of 1812 hypothecation became an accepted practice in the United States.

Letter Stock: Such stock, which is not registered with the SEC, usually is sold privately by the issuing corporation to a purchaser who states in a letter that he is taking the stock for investment and not for distribution or resale. Some institutions have made heavy purchases of letter stock from the issuing company at a price lower than they could buy unrestricted stock on the open market. But, because of the investment letter requirement, letter stock is not liquid. Some mutual funds have been at fault, in my judgment, in giving their letter stock the same market value as the company's unrestricted stock.

Limited Partnership: In this form of organization, some partners have a liability limited to the amount of their investment in the business. To establish this limited liability, public notice of it must be given. There must also be at least one general partner who is fully liable for all claims on the business.

Limited liability attracts capital contributions from persons who would otherwise hesitate to become partners. It also appeals to persons unwilling or unable to participate in the firm's management. In addition, limited liability makes it possible for an elderly partner to withdraw from active participation but still retain an investment without having all his assets at risk. Many New York Stock Exchange firms are limited partnerships.

Margin Buyers: Such buyers do not put up the full purchase price of their stock, but put up a portion of the price. The limit of the percentage is determined by the Federal Reserve Board, which changes this limit from time to time. At the present writing, the margin limit is 55%, having just been lowered by the Federal Reserve Board from its previous level of 65%. It stood at 80% in May 1970. To some it appeared that the reduction from 80% to 65% came about as a consequence of the intervention of the Administration following the April 29 meeting described in Chapter II.

Margin Calls: Calls are made by brokers to customers when the market value of the securities in a customer's margin account drops below legally permissible levels set by the New York Stock Exchange, presently 25% of their value. (At Merrill Lynch, the level is 30%.) Obviously, the value of a customer's equity in his stock goes down when the price drops. The broker who has financed the margin account then requires that the customer put up sufficient cash so that he has enough equity in his account to meet the minimum requirement.

Margin Regulations: The amount of credit a person or firm may obtain when buying stocks is regulated by the Federal Reserve Board. On July 8, 1969, the Board of Governors of the Federal Reserve System ruled that some 400 over-the-counter stocks could be bought on margin, subject to the same rules and limitations governing stocks listed on the national exchanges. The over-the-counter stocks that were selected were generally good quality stocks, with the same characteristics as stocks registered on national exchanges. This meant that a person or firm buying stock on credit at that time would have to put up at least 80% of the total purchase price and could obtain credit for the remainder. The margin requirement has since been cut twice: to 65% and then to 55%. Since 1945, margin rates have fluctuated in a range between 50 and 100%, depending upon market conditions and the Fed's response to them.

Money Supply or Money Stock: In the most widely accepted definition, demand deposits (checking accounts in commercial banks) plus money in circulation equal the money stock. However, one financial economist a few years ago said, "Everyone rolls his own definition of money and has his own rules for definition of the money supply." A broader definition would include time deposits at commercial banks, as well as demand deposits and currency, and a still broader definition adds deposits of mutual savings banks and savings and loan shares. These three concepts of the money supply (or "money stock") are referred to in the trade as M1, M2 and M3.

Moving Average: The average of sales volume over a period of time forms a continuing series on a chart, establishing a trend line. Because a single large contract, for example in the construction industry, could distort the figures for the month to which it applied, economists often use a three-month moving average to smooth out the results. Thus, to obtain a working figure for June, the economist will average the monthly figures for May, June and July. To get the figure for July, he will average June, July and August. By plotting such a continuing series on a chart, he can obtain a smoother and frequently more meaningful line.

In the stock market some security analysts favor a moving average that covers 200 days as an indicator of longer-term movements. They add up the closing prices of a stock on 200 consecutive days, then divide by 200 to get the moving average for the 200th day. On the 201st day, Day Number 1 is dropped, and the price for Day Number 201 is added. And so it continues.

National Association of Securities Dealers, Inc.: This is a nonprofit, self-regulatory membership organization of over-the-counter brokers and dealers authorized in 1938 under provisions of the Maloney Act, an amendment to the Securities Exchange Act of 1934. Its purpose is national regulation of the over-the-counter securities market. The NASD was registered with the SEC in 1939. Since they had not been nationally organized as a unit, OTC dealers were not subject to the same control that stock exchanges exercised over their members. The NASD provided the instrument for accomplishing that control. It became the first truly national organization of brokers and dealers embracing the whole industry without regard to location, the kind or volume of business done, or collateral affiliations. In 1971 the NASD had approximately 4,000 members.

New York Call Money Rate: This is the rate of interest banks charge for loans made in a sector of the money market known as the call money market. In this market, brokers and dealers are loaned money, secured by stocks and bonds and Government securities, to meet their money requirements for carrying customers' margin accounts and their own inventories. New York banks are the chief suppliers of this form of credit. Thus the rate is called the New York call money rate. The call loan rate is usually the same as the prime interest rate.

New York Stock Exchange Composite Index: This computation of price movements of all common stocks traded on the New York Stock Exchange was set up in answer to complaints that the Dow Jones Index was too narrow and selective to be an accurate measure of the market's performance. Also, the electronic computation of an index that reflects the price movements of all N.Y.S.E. common stocks became possible. The N.Y.S.E. Composite index, which covers every common stock listed on the Exchange, has been computed on a daily close basis since May 28, 1964. Group indexes—Industrial, Transportation, Utility and Finance—have been computed on a daily close basis beginning with 1966. And since mid-1966, the Composite has been computed every half-hour and the group indexes every hour.

New York Stock Exchange Revenues: The Exchange's income principally comes from the fees charged members for the use of tickers and for stock clearing services. In 1970 these fees amounted to $29.2-million. Commission charges and fees for odd-lot dealer transactions brought in another $13.5-million. Listing fees paid by corporations that list on the Exchange added $13.8-million. The Exchange's total income was $69,333,000. It had a loss of $12.7-million, because of financial contributions made to reimburse customers of bankrupt member firms.

New York Times Stock Averages: These are daily averages of 25 industrial stocks and 25 rails, computed separately and as a composite. The method used by the *Times* to compensate for stock splits is to apply a multiplier to the price of a split stock equal to the split ratio. For example, if a previously unsplit stock should split 3-for-one, the *Times* would give it a permanent multiplier of 3. If the same stock subsequently split 2-for-1, the multiplier would become 6. Some stocks in the averages have been split so often they have high multipliers: Caterpillar Tractor has a multiplier of 60, and so does Eastman Kodak. General Motors' multiplier is six. The closing price of the industrials is multiplied by the multiplier for that stock, the totals are added, and that figure is divided by 25, giving the industrial average for the day. The same process is followed for the 25 rail stocks. The two indexes are then added, and that total is divided by two, giving the composite average.

Open Market Committee of the Federal Reserve Board: This vitally important committee buys and sells Government bonds in the open market. To give an idea of volume, in September 1969—a busy week—the Committee sold as much as $4-billion in bonds. This, of course, affects the amount of money in circulation. When the Fed buys bonds, it injects money into the economy; when it sells them, it soaks money up. Thus it can either enlarge or contract the money supply. But the decisions and dealings of the Open Market Committee, alas, are secret until 90 days after its decisions are taken.

Over-the-counter Market: On this market are traded thousands of securities which are not listed on a major securities market. They are traded in direct negotiation between buyers and sellers, and this face-to-face feature led to the over-the-counter name for the system. Traders generally specialize in a number of stocks, acting as intermediary between buyers and sellers or acting on their own account, making a market in the stocks. The OTC is the principal market for United States Government bonds and municipals and, until recently, was also the chief market for all banks and insurance companies, a number of which are now on the New York Stock Exchange. Other companies represented on the OTC are those with too few stockholders, too little outstanding stock or too brief an earnings record to qualify for listing on the large exchanges. As NASDAQ now reveals, the volume of common stock traded over-the-counter is greater than volume on any exchange except the New York Stock Exchange.

Par Value: This is the nominal value of a share of corporate stock. To arrive at it, the total stated capital stock is divided by the number of shares authorized; a corporation with a $1-million capital and issuing 20,000 shares, for example, places a $50 par value on each share. An accounting term relating to the general capitalization of the company, par value has nothing to do with the market value of the stock. Par values can range from one cent to $100. Par value as an indication of the value of a security does not have the importance it once had. Virtually no states make a stated par value a requirement for stock issuance.

On the bond market, however, par has a different meaning. It stands for $1,000. When Wall Street says that a bond is selling at "par to a quarter," it means that while $1,000 is bid for the bond, it is offered at $1,002.50.

Productivity: Output per man-hour, or the amount of goods produced divided by the total number of man-hours consumed in producing it, equals productivity. Productivity is very hard to measure in the service sector of the economy.

Recession, Depression: These are terms used to describe various degrees of slowdown in the economy. Recession is usually accepted as being two or more successive quarters with no real gain in the Gross National Product. On the basis of that definition the economic troubles in 1969–70 as reflected in the drop in the GNP—in constant dollars—qualified as a recession. Depression, on the other hand, is defined by some as a phase in the business cycle featured by excessive unemployment, subnormal prices and business activity, drastically curtailed production, lower incomes, a declining stock market and widespread pessimism.

Refundings: There are three main obligations of the United States Treasury—United States Government bonds, notes and bills. Each has a different life span. When one of these obligations comes due, the Treasury offers to replace that obligation with another one due at a later date. Sometimes these refundings are very large, as the one that took place in June 1970, which amounted to $641-million. But that was nowhere near a record. During July of 1964, there was a $41.8-billion refunding.

Registered Representative: He is the full-time employee of a New York Stock Exchange member firm who executes customer's orders in the trading of securities. To qualify, registered representatives have to meet New York Exchange requirements, including passing tests of their knowledge of the securities market.

Back in the 1920s and 1930s, a registered representative was known as a "customer's man." There were few qualifications for the job then. Graduates of Harvard, Yale and Princeton were in great demand regardless of their competence. Later the terms "customer's broker" and "registered representative" came into use. In 1933 the Stock Exchange approved a questionnaire designed to test applicants for such jobs on their knowledge of market procedures and Exchange regulations. Applicants were later required to pass certain courses of study at the New York Institute of Finance or a similar institution. Successful completion of the course was considered an adequate substitute for passing the New York Stock Exchange's exam. Since 1962, though, the New York Stock Exchange has required candidates to pass its own written examination in all cases.

Reserve Requirements: Federal Reserve member banks must keep these required legal reserves against their time and demand deposits. Congress gives the Federal Reserve Board power to raise or lower the required ratio within certain limits. If the Fed wants to reduce the money supply, it can raise the required reserve ratios, currently 17% for deposits under $5-million, and 17½% for deposits over $5-million, on the demand deposits of city reserve banks (larger banks), and 12½% and 13% respectively on the demand deposits of country (smaller) reserve banks. Reserves against time deposits are 3% on savings deposits; 3% on other time deposits under $5-million; and 5% on other time deposits over $5-million. If the Fed desires to ease credit, it can lower the ratio.

To change reserve requirements is to use a powerful tool. For instance, if the Board were to raise requirements from, let's say, 20% to 25% (an extreme example), banks would have to add to their reserves and decrease their deposits until the ratio of deposits to reserves was 4 to 1 instead of 5 to 1. This would involve calling in loans, limiting new loans and probably selling bonds.

Secondary Distribution: In this form of underwriting, a selling group or syndicate offers a block of stock (not a new issue) after the close of the market at a fixed price, not exceeding the last sale price on the floor. Once a favored means of disposing of large outstanding issues, it has been less used recently. Some believe it is coming back in style.

Selling Climax: This is the nadir that professionals look for toward the end of a steadily declining market. Like other events on Wall Street, however, a selling climax is hard to recognize while it is going on; only some months, or even years, after the event can one be sure that one has lived through it. Still, after the market has been drifting down further and further over a lengthy period, a time usually comes along when quite a few people—and these may be the hard-bitten technicians as well as those weaker in spirit— begin to get discouraged and act on their mood. They begin to dump their shares—to sell them at whatever the going market price is, as quickly as they can.

That of course increases volume as prices decrease, or to use the shorthand of the Street, "volume picks up on the downside." Then at some point floor traders—those people who own seats on the Exchange and trade there for their own accounts to save paying commissions to a broker—and others, possibly institutional investors running performance funds and looking for a quick turn, begin to see opportunities amid the shambles. Quite suddenly, they decide their moment has come. They jump in to buy. The course of the race is reversed. Instead of sellers chasing buyers, buyers suddenly start to chase sellers. The market quickly turns around and "it runs away on the upside."

All of that sounds quite simple, but, of course, it's not so clear at the time. What is happening may not really be a selling climax but only a temporary reversal in the fall of prices, which will be promptly resumed in the next few hours or whenever trading resumes. A true selling climax can be identified only in retrospect—unfortunately.

Short Sale: The investor sells borrowed stock, which he must return at a later date. The investor's hope is that when the later date comes he will be able to buy the stock for less than he sold it for, and he can pocket the difference. Actually, the customer's broker borrows the stock for him from someone else and makes delivery to the buyer.

If one were to sell a stock short at 50 and it were to fall to 40, at that point one could buy to replace the stock borrowed and make $10 a share. On the other hand, if the stock were to go up to 60, it would have to be replaced at that price, at a loss of $10 a share. Some people believe that short selling is riskier than buying a stock for appreciation. If you buy a stock for appreciation, all you can lose is the amount of your original investment. But on a short sale, your potential loss is unlimited, since the stock you sold short could theoretically continue to rise indefinitely. This theoretical argument has never discouraged short sellers in the past. As explained in the text, the day comes when what has been borrowed must be replaced. Short sellers often rush to buy stocks when stocks appear to be headed upward, to cut their potential losses.

Specialist–Specialist's Post: The specialist is a member of the Stock Exchange who specializes in a limited number of stocks in which he is expected to maintain an orderly market by matching buy and sell orders and, to some extent, by buying or selling for his own account to stabilize the stock prices. He executes orders for other brokers when these have orders to buy or sell at specified prices; he can hold these in his book until he can match them. Numerous regulatory requirements limit the activities of specialists. They cannot, for instance, recommend or publicize, orally or in writing, the purchase or sale of any stock in which they specialize, nor solicit, buy or sell orders in these. These restrictions apply also to the specialist's firm. On the floor, the specialist is distinguished by having a set position, or post, where he conducts business.

Standard & Poor's Indexes: Stock price indexes are compiled by Standard & Poor's Corporation and computed at half-hour intervals during each trading day. The Composite Index includes 500 New York Stock Exchange common stocks (425 industrials, 20 railroads and 55 utilities), with indexes computed also for these three major groups. The 500 stocks, plus a number of unlisted companies, are further subdivided into 100 industry groups for which weekly indexes are available.

The formula used to produce the S&P indexes is known as a "base-weighted aggregative," expressed in ratios with the average value for the base period (1941–43) equal to 10. In effect, this formula gives weight to each stock in proportion to the market value of all the outstanding shares of that stock.

The major Standard & Poor indexes (composite, industrials, rails, utilities) date back to 1918.

Technician: This securities analyst follows the movements of stocks through the use of graphs, charts, and computers. He analyzes trends, momentum, and evidence of "accumulation" and "distribution." In addition to their study of prices and volume, many technicians factor in studies of market psychology and the total environment for stocks. This includes the study of money flows and other evidence that relates to the movements of prices of stock, such as the Federal Reserve's monetary policy, the trend in interest rates, and an evaluation of earnings. Historical cycles and past market patterns also play their role. Technical analysts use exotically-named types of charts ("head and shoulders") and search them for special patterns ("point and figures").

This kind of analysis, which is mathematically very complex, is obviously not an exact science. Sometimes it takes on a bit of the magic of astrology. But good technicians are vital to good research.

INDEX

211